FRANCIS

Andrea Tornielli

FRANCIS

Pope of a New World

Translated by
William J. Melcher

IGNATIUS PRESS   SAN FRANCISCO

Original Italian edition
Jorge Mario Bergoglio. Francesco Insieme
© 2013 by Edizioni Piemme Spa, Milan, Italy

Cover photo
Pope Francis Waves to the Crowd from Balcony of St. Peter's Basilica
Wednesday, March 13, 2013
© AP Photo / Dmitry Lovetsky

Cover design by John Herreid

To my mother, Eleonora

Contents

Foreword

by Father Mitch Pacwa, S.J.

In my adult years as a priest, the Chair of Peter has been filled four times. The election of John Paul I evoked the usual joy of having a new Holy Father and the hope that the Church might find stability at a time of theological and liturgical turmoil. However, I did not feel particular engagement with the new pope. The shock thirty days later when he died actually made a deeper impression on me than had his election.

The election of his successor got my attention, and I remember well that a radio was broadcasting in the background as I studied, waiting for the announcement of a new pope. When the news-caster said that Karol Wojtyła of Kraków, Poland, was now Pope John Paul II, I raced down the three flights of stairs, perhaps touching a few of them as I ran, carrying a box of chocolates to pass out on the street as I gleefully announced to every passerby, "The new pope is Polish!" Excitement that a Pole had been chosen swelled my heart with ethnic pride and joy, making Polish jokes and slurs in the past fade into insignificance. However, the twenty-seven-year reign far exceeded ethnic hopes, as his vigor captured everyone's attention and a whole new approach to philosophy and theology fired an enthusiasm for the truth of the Catholic faith. From his first year as pope, vocations began to increase and a generation of clergy, religious, and laity would be known as the John Paul II generation. Dissidents on the theological right and left huddled among themselves as Catholicism swelled to a new force in the modern world under John Paul's leadership.

In 2005, I watched the advance of Pope Benedict XVI to Saint Peter's balcony with a deeper joy, since it meant that another extraordinary teacher would continue to guide the Church, leaving theological and liturgical confusion farther behind. He focused on Jesus Christ as he quietly, humbly led the Church forward, retaining the love and allegiance of the John Paul generation.

Pope Benedict's retirement came as a jolt but not as a total surprise. His age had advanced, and his strength had waned. This book presents many key insights into Pope Benedict's retirement, and every Catholic will appreciate the mature assessment of a decision that raised much speculation and less wisdom from various pundits inside and outside the Church.

In 2013, the election of Pope Francis evoked another kind of pride—a fellow Jesuit, the first one in history, had been elected pope. Certainly Jesuits had spoken of him, since he was not only an archbishop in an important archdiocese, Buenos Aires, Argentina, but also a cardinal. The Constitutions of the Society of Jesus prohibit Jesuits from seeking to be bishops, but the pope can override that rule and choose a Jesuit to belong to the college of bishops, as happened to Father Jorge Bergoglio, S.J. Vague rumors circulated that he was a *papabile* after John Paul II died, but most Jesuits I knew dismissed them with the generally accepted assumption that a Jesuit would never be pope. I remembered him from 2005, but I thought he might be past the age being sought for a new pope in 2013, since so many people were speaking about the importance of a young pope for the modern world. However, neither his age nor his being a Jesuit hindered him, and Jorge Bergoglio, S.J., walked out on the balcony of Saint Peter's as Pope Francis.

As I watched this drama develop, my pride was not exuberant, as when the Pole Karol Wojtyła emerged, but quiet. I stood in the EWTN studio with Franciscan friars, cameramen, fellow hosts waiting to comment, and visitors who formed an audience. Their congratulations to me as a Jesuit could not change my silence; text messages began pouring into my phone, but it was not a time to accept congratulations, especially since I had done nothing but follow the gift of my Jesuit vocation as Pope Francis had done even longer than I.

A peaceful joy deepened as this new pope's personality unfolded before the crowd in Saint Peter's Square, the whole world, and us in the studio. His simple "Good evening", his light comments about being the Bishop of Rome, and especially his bow toward us, that we all might pray for him and bless him before he blessed us for the first time as pope, were a triumph of quiet joy. This moment was followed by many small moments of making ordinary actions quite uncommon—riding a bus with the cardinals, praying alone at Saint Mary Major, stopping to pay his bill in person at a Rome hotel for priests, calling the man who delivered his papers in Buenos Aires to cancel the subscription, meeting with the Jesuit Father General Adolfo Nicolás, S.J., to accept his offer of Jesuit support to the new pope, and the Pope's extension of his apostolic blessing to all Jesuits and those who work with them. These moments stream forth from him, making his office yet more amazing.

Where does all this come from in Pope Francis? What led to the election of a Latin American Jesuit as pope? What is the background against which his first papal acts find their context? Certainly his family is essential, and in this book we get a first glimpse of the people who raised him and their attitudes toward his Jesuit vocation. We learn how the Lord called him from his first career choice to a Jesuit vocation that could incorporate those same talents in ministry rather than career. We will understand the development of his Jesuit life in a period of turmoil and change in the Church and during extraordinarily difficult political circumstances, as the Argentinian government swung to the violent right and a secular left that opposed Church teaching. What were the constants in Padre Jorge Bergoglio's ministry and service as a Jesuit and as an archbishop in violent, horrible times? These questions are addressed in this book. In addition, there is invaluable background on Pope Benedict's resignation and the process of electing Pope Francis. May this knowledge of Pope Francis' past and background enlighten every reader, not so much as to make the new pope predictable within the confines of the categories stemming from his personal history, but to provide a context for the new surprises he seems capable of offering to the Church and to the modern world as a whole.

Introduction

"I ask you to pray for me ..."

On Wednesday, March 13, 2013, after having witnessed the black smoke in the late morning and eaten my usual meal of vegetables and grilled calamari with my colleagues at Roberto's restaurant along the Passetto di Borgo, I left the Vatican to return to the editorial offices of *La Stampa* on the via Barberini. Ever since newspapers became multimedia websites as well, print journalists have also had to do live television broadcasts and audio-video service. "If there is white smoke this evening," the boss had told me, "we must immediately do a live streaming broadcast and commentary on the announcement ..." The cardinals had been shut up in the Vatican for about a day, without any possibility of communicating with the outside; the forecasts of the newspapers and of the various purple-robed prelates spoke about a "difficult" and "uncertain" conclave, which would certainly be longer than the one in 2005 that had elected Joseph Ratzinger. For lack of a strong candidate like the Prefect of the Congregation for the Doctrine of the Faith eight years ago, one capable of galvanizing a consensus, the selection of the 266th Bishop of Rome would therefore be longer and more laborious.

And yet that very day a dear friend and colleague of mine, Gerard O'Connell, had forewarned me: "In my opinion, there could be a pope this evening ..." That morning I had left the house with a little book in my bag: *El Jesuita*, the book-length interview with the Cardinal of Buenos Aires written by Sergio Rubin and Francesca Ambrogetti. Of all the *papabili* in the conclave, Cardinal Bergoglio was the one I knew best. I had interviewed him only once, in February 2012, for *Vatican Insider*, a thematic website of *La Stampa*, but for several years I had had the opportunity to meet him during his rare trips to Rome. I had spoken several times with him about the life of the Church. I had become acquainted with and even hosted in my house in Rome Padre Pepe, one of his priests who proclaim the Gospel in the *villas miserias*, the shanty-towns of Buenos Aires.

What always struck me about Bergoglio was his profound faith vision, his humility, his words, which were able to reach people's hearts and help them receive the embrace of God's mercy. On occasion I have submitted to him articles or reflections published on my blog, but I have also asked him for prayers. At the end of every encounter, his unfailing request was: "Pray for me, I ask you to pray for me ..."

Since I live, when in Rome, next door to my lifelong friends Gianni Valente and Stefania Falasca, I have also been able to witness the ties of friendship between their family and Padre Bergoglio. I, too, have been able to listen to his stories, his experiences as a pastor, his encounters with the faithful who have loved him so much, because in him they recognize one of themselves: someone who came to serve and not to lord it over them. A man who came to share, not merely to exercise a sacred authority. Someone who came to attract with his merciful smile, not to "regulate the faith". A man who came to facilitate their encounter with Jesus. Nearness, mercy, gentleness, patience: these are the words of Father Bergoglio—a pastor who has related that his greatest sorrow as a bishop was to learn that "some priests do not baptize the children of unwed mothers because they were not conceived within the sanctity of marriage."

I had seen him extremely calm in the days leading up to the conclave. "At night I sleep like a baby", he had confided to Gianni and Stefania. He had told us that he had already prepared his homily for Holy

Thursday, which he would read upon returning to Buenos Aires; he had spoken to us about his return flight, already booked for March 23, and about an appointment with the Jewish community that he did not want to miss. "I must return to my Spouse", he kept saying, referring to his diocese with a smile on his face—this bishop who truly considered the Church of Buenos Aires as a wife, loving and serving her in everything and in everyone, starting with the poorest. These were not the kind of remarks that are made almost superstitiously by someone who is trying to exorcise an impending responsibility. These were stories about the life of a simple man.

Yet never before, it seemed to me in the days leading up to the start of the conclave, had I noticed in Cardinal Bergoglio such serenity and abandonment to the will of God, whatever the plan he was preparing might be.

Maybe that was also why, on the afternoon of March 13, as soon as I arrived at the office, I began to write precisely about him, while listening several times with headphones to a musical selection that I find particularly relaxing, the famous Canon in D Major by Pachelbel, performed by the London Symphony Orchestra. It so happened once that I heard it performed on the harp while I was with Padre Bergoglio and other friends. Then, at 4:05 P.M., after a gull had repeatedly perched on the copper chimney coping on the roof of the Sistine Chapel, lo and behold, the very first puffs of white smoke. They had elected a pope. Together with my colleague Paolo Mastrolilli, I had to conduct a live streaming video session for the website of *La Stampa*. We waited for the announcement while telling web-surfers what was about to happen. When Cardinal Jean-Louis Tauran had pronounced the prophetic words, "Habemus Papam" and began to pronounce the initial syllable "Geo ..." of Georgium, I shouted: "Bergoglio!" I began to tell something about him, about his life, his story, his way of being a bishop, his simplicity and humility, his critique of the "spiritual worldliness" of the Church.

"How did you manage to keep from crying during the live broadcast? We were all crying ...", my wife asked me from Milan, via Skype, when I was finally able to listen to her.

The simplicity of Pope Francis, his profound gesture of bowing his head to receive the blessing invoked on him by his people, his spontaneous greeting—"Buona sera", "Good evening"—and the fact that he continued to be himself and nothing more, even as Bishop of Rome and Pontiff, made an impression on the hearts of millions of believers.

He did not want the red *mozzetta* (cape) lined with ermine or the red shoes. He did not want to change his poor iron cross or his very modest ring.

The day afterward, he went to pray before the image of *Maria Salus populi romani* (Mary, Welfare of the Roman people) at the Basilica of Saint Mary Major without being accompanied by the pomp of a retinue or by an impressive security detail, which too often runs the risk of making the Bishop of Rome, a pastor, appear in the eyes of the faithful like the president of a superpower. Father Bergoglio, Pope Francis, the first Jesuit pope, the first Latin American, the first to take for himself the name of the great Saint of Assisi, with his little yet grand gestures and his words, at the dawn of his pontificate, is already making people understand what it means today to profess Jesus Christ.

"Let us never yield to pessimism," he said while meeting the cardinals in the Sala Clementina, "let us never yield to that bitterness which the devil offers us every day; let us not yield to pessimism or discouragement: let us be quite certain that the Holy Spirit bestows upon the Church, with his powerful breath, the courage to persevere and also to seek new methods of evangelization, so as to bring the Gospel to the uttermost ends of the earth." And on the evening of March 13, the world had a clear testimony to it.

1

Habemus Papam Franciscum

Saint Peter's Square is an enormous expanse of open umbrellas. Thousands of people, braving the cold and the rain, had been waiting for hours for the copper chimney of the Sistine Chapel to give the expected response. On the first evening, at 4:30 P.M., the long, impressive procession of 115 purple-garbed prelates, the electors of the conclave that had been called to appoint the successor of Benedict XVI, filed from the Pauline Chapel to the Sistine. After the oath [of secrecy] and the meditation presented by Cardinal Prosper Grech, the cardinals voted for the first time. Even though a result of black smoke was taken for granted, many, many people had gathered with their noses held high, waiting to know the outcome. The abundant billows of raven-colored smoke confirmed that the electors had decided to start immediately with the ballots. And, as was to be expected, none of them had won the seventy-seven votes necessary, equivalent to two-thirds.

On Wednesday, March 13, after an initial whitish puff, the smoke at midday had been grayish-black, too, following the two ballots of the morning, that is, the second and third votes of the conclave. In this case, too, a rather predictable outcome. In the last hundred years, only Eugenio Pacelli had been elected on the third ballot, in March 1939. (At that time, war was imminent, and the cardinals hastily chose Pope Ratti's faithful Secretary of State.) Outside, the crowds, both of the media and of the faithful and the curious, were wondering what was going on beneath the roof of the Sistine Chapel, in front of that dramatic, stupendous fresco of the *Last Judgment* by Michelangelo. Or what was happening among the cardinals during lunch in the Domus Sanctae Marthae, where they were staying. As of that afternoon, an election began to become more likely, despite the predictions of a long, difficult conclave. For Joseph Ratzinger, in April 2005, it had happened that way. He had been elected on the fourth ballot.

That afternoon, however, the first vote, too, had been inconclusive. There had been no sign of white smoke between 5:00 and 6:00 P.M. And so this meant that the cardinals had continued with another vote, the fourth of the day, the fifth of the conclave. The smoke, either white or black, was expected around 7:00 P.M. A few minutes before then, a seagull had perched on top of the chimney, and he had been seen to remain there, immobile, for more than half an hour, appearing also on the four big screens positioned on the square in front of the Vatican Basilica.

"That is not a good sign," said one priest, "because the bird that symbolizes the Spirit is the dove, certainly not the seagull. It means they have not yet decided." And yet there was something that people were paying attention to. A growing expectation for which there was no external or human reason.

At 7:05 P.M., white smoke that was at first almost transparent and then increasingly dense and immaculate began to issue from the chimney, a visible sign alerting the crowd, which started to applaud. The pope was elected, even though the world still did not know his name and his face. At last, at that very moment, it stopped raining. The wait seemed endless. Then, finally, the great curtains of the central *loggia* (balcony) of Saint Peter's opened, and the Cardinal Proto-Deacon Jean-Louis Tauran appeared before the crowd to announce the name of the newly elected pope: "Annuntio vobis gaudium magnum, habemus Papam, Eminentissimum ac Reverendissimum Dominum Georgium Marium, Sanctae Romanae Ecclesiae Cardinalem Bergoglio, qui sibi nomen imposuit Franciscum."

"Georgium Marium" would have been enough to understand that the man elected was the Cardinal of Buenos Aires, a Jesuit archbishop born in that city seventy-six years before, of a family of emigrants from the Piedmont.

The name was unknown, and, at first, the people remained somewhat disconcerted. (Just as on another evening, that of October 16, 1978, when Cardinal Pericle Felici announced to the faithful that the new pope was Karol Wojtyła.) Padre Bergoglio, then. Everyone was expecting a young pontiff, and instead the cardinals had turned around and chosen one who was already old. Many were making predictions about the "Italian pope", and instead the new Bishop of Rome arrived from the Southern Hemisphere of the world, from a far-off land. After retracing in the opposite direction the voyage that his family had made in 1929 when they embarked at the port of Genoa.

Anyone who knows Bergoglio, his stature, his episcopate, immediately perceived the import of the event. This was made evident also by his choice of name: Francis. Upon hearing that name, the crowd burst into resounding applause. A Jesuit pope who took the name of the *Poverello* of Assisi, founder of the Franciscans. A sign of change, of a turning point. The call to be radically evangelical, a poor Church that journeys, builds, and professes Christ crucified, "the one Savior of all mankind and of all men".

A few more minutes passed, and lo and behold, the new pope appeared. It was only 8:10 P.M. For the first time in history, before the newly elected pope went out onto the balcony, a snippet of video by the Vatican Television Center showed Francis clothed in white vestments while waiting at the window. The pontiff was not wearing the red *mozzetta* lined with ermine that had been prepared, nor did he have the stole over his shoulders. Later we would learn that he did not want to use that regal garment trimmed with fur. The pectoral cross was not changed; it was the one that Jorge Mario Bergoglio always carried with him. It is made of plain metal, not gold. It is not set with any precious stones.

The new pope emerged, surrounded by masters of ceremony and several cardinals; he wanted to have at his side the Vicar of Rome, Agostino Vallini. No sooner had he come out than he made a sign of greeting by raising his right hand, and then he remained immobile, looking toward the square. Without saying a thing, while the crowd applauded and shouted "Viva il papa!" Then finally he spoke and said: "Brothers and sisters, good evening . . ." A simple greeting, which recalled the last words of Benedict XVI, pronounced a moment before going back into the papal palace of Castel Gandolfo to remain "hidden from the world".

Francis continued: "You know that it was the duty of the Conclave to give Rome a Bishop. It seems that my brother Cardinals have gone to the ends of the earth to get one ... but here we are ... I thank you for your welcome. The diocesan community of Rome now has its Bishop. Thank you! And first of all, I would like to offer a prayer for our Bishop Emeritus, Benedict XVI. Let us pray together for him, that the Lord may bless him and that Our Lady may keep him."

He did not describe himself as pope, but recalled at first that he is Bishop of Rome, as, incidentally, John Paul II had done in his first appearance after his election. The pope is pope because he is Bishop of Rome, and not vice versa, as some individuals who exalt the splendor of the papal court sometimes seem to forget. Pope Bergoglio underscored this special, particular bond with the Church of the Eternal City. He was a bishop who spoke to the members of his diocese before addressing the world.

Then, right afterward, Francis invited the people to pray for his predecessor, and together with the faithful he recited the Our Father, the Hail Mary, and the Glory be. He had the people pray, he had them recite the most frequently used prayers in the Christian faith.

"And now," he began to speak again after finishing the three prayers, "we take up this journey: Bishop and People. This journey of the Church of Rome, which presides in charity over all the Churches. A journey of fraternity, of love, of trust among us. Let us always pray for one another. Let us pray for the whole world, that there may be a great spirit of fraternity. It is my hope for you that this journey of the Church, which we start today, and in which my Cardinal Vicar, here present, will assist me, will be fruitful for the evangelization of this most beautiful city."

It was the moment for the blessing, the first apostolic blessing; the new pope had just asked the people to be blessed. He asked the people to pray for God's blessing on their new bishop. An entirely new and unheard-of request, which sees the laity as playing a leading role, the people of God with their prayer for their new pastor.

"And now I would like to give the blessing, but first I ask a favor of you: before the Bishop blesses his people, I ask you to pray to the Lord that he will bless me: the prayer of the people asking the blessing for their Bishop. Let us make, in silence, this prayer: your prayer over me."

Francis bowed his head, then spoke again and said: "Now I will give the Blessing to you and to the whole world, to all men and women of good will." He put on the papal stole over his white habit and bestowed the blessing in Latin, granting the plenary indulgence "Urbi et Orbi" (to the City and to the World). Then, after saluting with a hand gesture, he asked for the microphone again and concluded: "Thank you for your welcome. Pray for me. And until we meet again. We will see each other soon. Tomorrow I wish to go and pray to Our Lady, that she may watch over all of Rome. Good night and sleep well!"

Having left the apostolic palace to return to Santa Marta, the Pope found himself in front of the big black car with the license plate "SCV 1" [Vatican City State #1]. But Francis did not take it. "I'll get on the bus with the cardinals . . ." He would do the same the following morning to return to the Sistine Chapel to concelebrate Mass with the purple-robed prelates.

They say that at dinner there was a festive, relaxed atmosphere. The Church finally had a new pope. The hundred fourteen temporary "prisoners" of the conclave had chosen a "prisoner" for life, the one who was to remain in the Vatican. Francis, greeting his confreres after dinner, looked at them and said, "May God forgive you for what you have done."

That same evening, the new pope telephoned the bishop emeritus, Benedict XVI. It is not the only telephone call he made. Francis also called some Roman friends at their home. And he immediately sent a message to the Chief Rabbi of Rome, Riccardo

Di Segni: "On this day of my election as Bishop of Rome and Pastor of the Universal Church, I send you my cordial greetings, informing you that the solemn inauguration of my pontificate will take place on Tuesday, March 19. Trusting in the protection of the Most High, I strongly hope to be able to contribute to the progress of the relations that have existed between Jews and Catholics since Vatican Council II in a spirit of renewed collaboration and in service of a world that may always be more in harmony with the Creator's will."

Francis began the first day of his pontificate as usual, rising very early to pray for a long time before the tabernacle. Then, as he had announced the previous evening, he intended to pray to Our Lady to keep and protect the Diocese of Rome. A little before eight, he appeared in the Basilica of Saint Mary Major for a private visit. In the large chapel in the left nave of the oldest church dedicated to Our Lady is preserved the image of *Salus Populi Romani*. The new pope entered, holding in one hand a bunch of flowers, and stopped to pray before the Marian icon. Then he went to the altar, beneath which is preserved a relic of the manger of the Nativity. Then to a chapel that is also called Sistine, to the altar where Saint Ignatius of Loyola celebrated his First Mass one Christmas Eve: it is a place fraught with symbolism for the Jesuits. Francis then prayed at the tomb of Saint Pius V, the pope of the Battle of Lepanto and of the Mass of the old rite—the Dominican pontiff, the one who inaugurated the tradition of white as the color for papal vestments because he wanted to keep his Dominican religious habit.

After praying, Francis met the staff, the cardinals present, and the Dominican confessors. "Mercy, mercy, mercy ..." This was his invitation to them as he greeted them one by one. "You are confessors, and therefore be merciful to souls. They need it", he added.

The new pope arrived in a car belonging to the Vatican police, not with the papal limousine. And he had an escort that was reduced to the minimum. The evening of his election, he had tried to speak with the director of the Domus Sacerdotalis Paulus VI, the house for clergy at via della Scrofa 70 in Rome, where he usually resided during his visits to the capital and where he had stayed for the two weeks before the conclave. On the days of the General Congregations, he always went on foot, both to and from.

The Pope notified the director that he would come by to pick up his luggage and his personal effects and to pay the bill. And so it was. Francis arrived in the former palace just a few steps from the Piazza Navona accompanied by the Prefect of the Papal Household, Archbishop Georg Gänswein, and, looking at their dismayed expressions, which seemed to

16

be trying to tell him, "Your Holiness, you are joking, you are really not going to pay?", he explained to them: "Precisely because I am the pope I must set an example."

Then he decided to go up to the room personally to collect his things, and he packed his suitcase himself. As he was accustomed to doing, incidentally, on every trip. Because Jorge Mario Bergoglio was always a bishop without a secretary. The pope who refuses the big sedan and the retinue, who prefers to ride with his "brother cardinals", who does not let anyone put ermine-trimmed garments on him, who does not think that he has risen to such a height as to prevent him from packing his bags himself and from demanding to pay the bill at the clergy house, like any other guest. So many little major signs. Today's world requires the Church to witness to the Gospel more by her life than by her words. And it should be normal for a Christian to behave with sobriety, with simplicity. Some displays of the Church Triumphant perhaps had significance in the past. Certainly today they appear out of date and not in keeping with modern sensibilities. And in some cases, they even run the risk of giving a contrary witness. Instead of bringing people closer, they drive them away. Pope Francis, by being himself through and through, attracts. As proved by the extraordinary reaction of so many, many people in the world who are

17

struck and fascinated by his extraordinary ordinariness and by his simplicity.

"Surely this pope will create an unprecedented problem for Vatican security", commented the Jesuit Father Federico Lombardi, director of the Vatican Press Office. He immediately added, however, "But those responsible for security are at the service of the Holy Father and know that they must adapt to his pastoral style."

The pope is not the one who has to adapt to certain exaggerated displays that in the name of security ran the risk of keeping Benedict XVI in a cage during the final years of his pontificate. The entourage are the ones who have to adapt to the style of the pontiff. A pontiff who is Bishop of Rome and who intends to establish a special relationship with his city and diocese.

2

If a Pope Resigns because of Old Age

Jorge Mario Bergoglio, Francis, is the first pope in the history of the Church to be elected successor of a pontiff who resigned because of old age. The events that brought a Jesuit Latin American bishop to the Throne of Peter began one Monday morning like so many others, February 11, 2013. That day, at 11:00 A.M., in the Consistory Hall, Benedict XVI had to preside at a public consistory for the canonization of several Blesseds. They were Antonio Primaldo and company (d. 1480), the martyrs of Otranto; Laura di Santa Caterina da Siena Montoya y Upegui (1874–1949), virgin, foundress of the Congregation of the Missionary Sisters of Mary Immaculate and of Saint Catherine of Siena; and Maria Guadalupe García Zavala (1878–1963), co-foundress of the Congregation of the Handmaids of Saint Margaret Mary (Alacoque) and the Poor. The Pope decreed that they should be "inscribed in the book of saints on Sunday, May 12, 2013".

Benedict XVI, however, did not stop there. He continued, reading a short statement in Latin that bore his signature and the date of the day before, in which he announced his decision to resign from the pontificate because of his age, declaring that the See of Peter would be vacant starting at 8:00 P.M. on February 28. Only at dawn on that Monday had the text been entrusted to the translators at the Secretariat of State, after they had been made to swear to keep the secret.

In a weak voice breaking with emotion, Pope Ratzinger said: "Conscientia mea iterum atque iterum coram Deo explorata ad cognitionem certam perveni vires meas ingravescente aetate non iam aptas esse ad munus Petrinum aeque administrandum."

"Dear Brothers," the Pope said in the presence of the astonished cardinals, who were utterly unprepared for what was about to happen, "I have convoked you to this Consistory, not only for the three canonizations, but also to communicate to you a decision of great importance for the life of the Church. After having repeatedly examined my conscience before God, I have come to the certainty that my strengths, due to an advanced age, are no longer suited to an adequate exercise of the Petrine ministry."

"I am well aware", added Benedict XVI, "that this ministry, due to its essential spiritual nature, must be carried out not only with words and deeds, but no less with prayer and suffering. However, in today's world, subject to so many rapid changes and shaken by questions of deep relevance for the life of faith, in order to govern the barque of Saint Peter and proclaim the Gospel, both strength of mind and body are necessary, strength which in the last few months, has deteriorated in me to the extent that I have had to recognize my incapacity adequately to fulfill the ministry entrusted to me."

"For this reason," the pontiff concluded, "and well aware of the seriousness of this act, with full freedom I declare that I renounce the ministry of Bishop of Rome, Successor of Saint Peter, entrusted to me by the Cardinals on 19 April 2005, in such a way that, as from 28 February 2013, at 8 P.M., the See of Rome, the See of Saint Peter, will be vacant and a Conclave to elect the new Supreme Pontiff will have to be convoked by those whose competence it is."

The Pope concluded by thanking the cardinals "most sincerely for all the love and work with which you have supported me in my ministry and I ask pardon for all my defects." He assured them that "I wish also to devotedly serve the Holy Church of God in the future through a life dedicated to prayer."

There are scarcely twenty-two lines in the Latin. Twenty-two lines destined to change the history of the Church. Immediately after reading them, Benedict XVI received the embrace of the Cardinal Deacon of the College of Cardinals, Angelo Sodano. Then with an uncertain gait, in silence, surrounded by the somber-faced prelates of the Papal Household, Ratzinger made his way back to the papal apartments, where he was to remain for another seventeen days. There, screened from indiscreet looks, he lost his composure and wept. Tears ran down the face of the weary old pope. The face of the first pope to resign in six centuries.

Benedict XVI, then, left the pontificate with an unprecedented announcement. His was a momentous choice, made in solitude. A choice that matured over time and was settled on his return from his March 2012 journey to Mexico and Cuba, as the editor of *L'Osservatore Romano*, Gian Maria Vian would write. During that trip, a success insofar as he had received a very warm welcome, the Pope had slipped during the night, causing a slight head injury.

Joseph Ratzinger had meditated on his decision for quite some time. He himself had spoken about the subject in 2010, in answering a question from a friend, the journalist Peter Seewald: "If a Pope clearly realizes that he is no longer physically, psychologically, and spiritually capable of handling the duties of his office, then he has a right and, under some circumstances, also an obligation to resign." Ratzinger had lived close to the Calvary of his predecessor, whose strength had been sapped by illness, and had already made it known then that he would not want that experience to be repeated. He would never want to be "managed" by those around him.

In October 2002, while still a cardinal, he had received from Archbishop Pasquale Macchi a copy of the letter with which Paul VI gave instructions to the cardinals in case of his prolonged incapacity, asking them to convoke the conclave. "This is something very wise that every pope ought to do", Ratzinger had commented when he looked over that photocopy. But the hypothetical case considered by Paul VI foresaw serious incapacity, and the end of Wojtyła's reign a disabling illness like Parkinson's disease. Nothing of the sort, in contrast, happened to Benedict XVI, who has arthritis and a weak heart.

"The Pope is not depressed, and there are no illnesses", his spokesman, Father Federico Lombardi, repeated. "There are no signs of decline", the papal physician, Patrizio Polisca, reiterated in those hours, alluding discreetly to his intellectual faculties, which remained intact, as the Pope had demonstrated

several days previously with an impromptu meditation in the presence of the Roman seminarians.

Then what happened? Why did Ratzinger, before
completing his eighty-sixth year, arrive at that momentous decision, knowing that it would cause an earth-
quake within and outside the Church? "The fact that
I suddenly found myself facing this tremendous task",
he had said in his interview with Seewald, "was ...
a shock for me. The responsibility is in fact enormous.... Yes, the thought of the guillotine occurred
to me: Now it falls down and hits you."

Ratzinger's pontificate was difficult. It seemed like
an obstacle course, a *via crucis*. Attacks, crises, scandals, like the overwhelming pedophilia scandal, which
the Pope confronted with a determination never
before recorded, but also tensions in governing the
Curia, factions, internal struggles. The difficulties and
the oppositions multiplied, some projects initiated
by the Pontiff ran aground, from the liturgical
"reform of the reform" to peace with the Lefeb-
vrites and the ecumenical dialogue. The Vatileaks
scandal brought to light a distressing reality that certainly cannot be reduced merely to the betrayal by
the majordomo Paolo Gabriele, as the three elderly,
trusted Cardinals Julián Herranz, Jozef Tomko, and
Salvatore De Giorgi were able to verify after Pope
Ratzinger commissioned them to conduct an internal investigation, the results of which have not been

revealed, not even to the cardinals before the conclave. The dossier in fact was delivered directly into the hands of the new Pope Francis.

Several times in recent years, Benedict XVI was compelled to intervene directly in order to shield his collaborators, whereas in the centuries-old tradition of the Church, it was always the reverse. The difficulties became too burdensome, and the weight of the pontificate was no longer tolerable.

Two decisions in the last months of the pontificate became easier to understand after the surprise announcement of the resignation: the little consistory in November 2012, with which the Pope, by appointing six new cardinals from different continents, "corrected" the preceding group of cardinals created in February, which was considered too curial and too Italian. The other sign was the appointment of his secretary, Georg Gänswein, as archbishop and Prefect of the Papal Household; obviously the Pope wanted to protect him in view of his now imminent resignation. Archbishop Gänswein now holds the twofold and unprecedented job of private secretary to the pope emeritus and Prefect of the Papal Household of the reigning pope.

Ratzinger's announcement caught almost everyone by surprise. The only ones who had been discreetly notified in advance were Cardinal Deacon Angelo Sodano and Secretary of State Tarcisio

Bertone. It was not a matter of consultations. The Pope had simply informed them of the decision that he had made "before God".

Benedict XVI waited to present his resignation for a period of relative calm after the Vatileaks disaster. A gesture of freedom and humility, which involved asking "pardon for all my defects", leaving no easy task to his successor. A gesture that contributed some-how to bringing even the papacy down to "normal" episcopal dimensions, with a Bishop Emeritus of Rome who retires to an apartment within the Vatican, liv-ing a life of prayer "hidden from the world". Within those walls—this had never happened—the new pon-tiff and his predecessor would now lodge. Rat-zinger's last surprise.

On April 24, 2005, during the Solemn Mass for the beginning of his service as Bishop of Rome, when Benedict XVI had asked the faithful to pray "that I may not flee out of fear from the wolves", no one could have imagined that his pontificate would be a *via crucis* and that it would end with the momentous gesture of his resignation.

Elected after a lightning-fast conclave that lasted less than a day, the seventy-eight-year-old Joseph Rat-zinger had made it clear from the start that his style would be different from that of his predecessor, for reasons of age and of training. The new pope did not want to present a "program of governance" because "my real program of governance is not to do my own will, not to pursue my own ideas, but to listen, together with the whole Church, to the word and the will of the Lord, to be guided by Him, so that He himself will lead the Church at this hour of our history."

Initially bashful and reserved, Ratzinger soon fell into the role of the traveling pope, starting from World Youth Day in Cologne in August 2005, one of the inventions of his volcanic predecessor. It had been his first great immersion in a crowd, the first test, which he passed thanks to effective messages and forceful images, like the one that compared the transformation of the bread and wine into the Body and Blood of Christ to nuclear fission. Although initially awkward in his gestures, Benedict XVI gave the best of himself in his improvised speeches, without the help of a written text, as in his meeting with the First Communion children on Saint Peter's Square on October 15, 2005, when the Pope had himself interviewed by them and answered one question about Jesus present but not visible in the Eucharist: "We do not see the electric current, and yet it exists and makes it possible for this microphone to function. . . . There are so many things that we do not see but that exist and are essential!"

Many had imagined that, given his age, the new pope would travel little. Instead, Ratzinger set about following in the footsteps of his predecessor. For instance, the journey to Poland in May 2006, which concluded with his visit to Auschwitz: "To speak in this place of horror, in this place where unprecedented mass crimes were committed against God and man, is almost impossible," he said, "and it is particularly difficult and troubling for a Christian, for a Pope from Germany. In a place like this, words fail; in the end, there can only be a dread silence—a silence which is itself a heartfelt cry to God: Why, Lord, did you remain silent? How could you tolerate all this?"

The year 2006 was also the year of the first international incident. Ratzinger likes to speak about the relationship between faith and reason, and during his trip to Bavaria, he once again donned the robes of a professor. He gave a lecture at his old university, in Regensburg, and an ancient citation about Muhammad, which the pontiff had not adopted as his own, was broadcast throughout the world and sparked protests in the Islamic world. From then on, Benedict XVI would increase the number of his signs of attention toward the Muslims and would stress friendship and respect toward Islam.

Although since his days as a cardinal he had often been branded as the *Panzerkardinal* (armored-tank cardinal), as Wojtyła's conservative inspiration, Ratzinger as pope continually spoke about the "joy of being Christian" and dedicated his first encyclical to the love of God, *Deus caritas est*. "Being Christian", he writes, "is not the result of an ethical choice or a lofty idea, but the encounter with an event, a Person, which gives life a new horizon and a decisive direction."

The theologian pope, before becoming the successor of John Paul II, dreamed of being able to retire, to leave the work of the Roman Curia so as to write a book about Jesus of Nazareth. And so, despite his new job, Ratzinger dedicated every free moment, especially vacations, to writing the work in three volumes that was published in 2007, 2011, and 2012. In addition to these three studies, there was also the book-length interview with Peter Seewald, *Light of the World*, the best thing to read in order to know who Joseph Ratzinger really is.

Benedict XVI faced difficult journeys; he confronted the galloping secularization of de-christianized societies and internal dissent in the Church. He celebrated his birthday at the White House together with George W. Bush, and several days later, on April 20, 2008, he prayed at Ground Zero while embracing relatives of the victims of the September 11 attacks.

Another serious crisis was the one that occurred in January 2009. The pope decided to lift the excommunications of the four bishops who had been consecrated by Archbishop Lefebvre. Among them

29

was Richard Williamson, who in a television interview a few months earlier had denied the existence of the gas chambers. Polemics exploded in the Jewish world; the Pope found himself alone and, faced with the obvious debacle of the curial apparatus of his collaborators, took up pen and paper and wrote to the bishops throughout the world, accepting all responsibility. There once was a time when collaborators in the Curia would shield the pope. With Ratzinger, exactly the reverse happened.

A year later, the pedophile scandal exploded again; documents were published about old cases that had been covered up, from the United States to Germany. There were even some who wanted to haul the Pontiff into court to answer for the crimes committed by the priests. Benedict XVI confronted the crisis squarely, without compromise, changing the rules and asking the Curia and the bishops of the world to change their mind-set. As a personal example, on every journey, he met with victims of pedophile priests. And during his flight to Portugal in May 2010, he went so far as to say that the most serious persecution for the Church comes not from her external enemies but from sin within the Church.

Some of the overtures that he made seeking reconciliation for the sake of Church unity were not understood and did not receive positive responses, such as liberalizing the norms for the celebration of the old preconciliar Mass and initiating dialogue with the Society of Saint Pius X. His final year was marked by leaks of confidential documents ("Vatileaks"), which caused tensions within the Vatican palaces to emerge and led to denunciations of incidents of corruption. Benedict XVI stayed calm and defended his co-workers with drawn sword, in the first place the Secretary of State, Cardinal Tarcisio Bertone, who was the object of more and more frequent attacks. He brought criminal proceedings against his majordomo, Paolo Gabriele, who confessed that he was guilty of having copied and circulated the papers. Then, however, before Christmas he visited him in prison and granted him pardon. Despite the fact that he had begun to celebrate the Year of Faith for the fiftieth anniversary of the opening of Vatican Council II, the Pope, whose priority was to proclaim the Gospel in its essential elements, left because he was weary. But not before he had got the successor of Peter on Twitter, as was fitting for a friend of modernity.

A resignation from the papacy is an extremely rare event in the history of the Church. The Bishops of Rome who abandoned their post are few, and until 2013 none of them had ever done so for reasons of age and health. Therefore, none of the cases in the past can be compared to what happened with Benedict XVI. At the very dawn of the Church, we find the case of Pope Clement, the third successor of Peter, after Linus and Anacletus, around the year 92. This was the pope who, according to tradition, authored a letter in which more generous souls are urged to step down rather than to give rise to division and discord. A statement that allegedly reflects the situation of the very person who wrote it.

The first documented case, however, is that of Pontian, the eighteenth bishop of Rome, elected around the year 230. Five years later, he was deported to Sardinia and condemned to forced labor in the mines. He resigned from office on September 28, 235, thus allowing Anterus to succeed him.

Three centuries would have to pass before arriving at Pope Silverius, son of Pope Hormisdas, subdeacon of the Church of Rome. He was placed on the throne in 536 by King Theodatus and dedicated himself to the battle against the Monophysites. Precisely this campaign of his caused the Empress Theodora anxiety, and she had him deported and banished to the island of Palmarona.

Several centuries passed, and we come to Benedict IX, who reigned from October 1032 to September 1044. The epitome of "absolute worldliness and the exploitation of papal authority", as *L'Osservatore Romano* has written, he was compelled to leave by a popular revolt. He managed to depose his successor, Silverius III, and returned to the throne for several weeks in 1045, before relinquishing the position again, this time to Gregory VI. He returned a third time to the throne, after the sudden death of Clement II, in October 1047, but was finally dismissed by Henry III, while continuing to consider himself the real pope in charge.

So we arrive at the great precedent of resignation, that of Celestine V, the hermit monk Pietro da Morrone, a canonized saint. He was elected pope in August 1294, was crowned in Aquila, and then withdrew to Naples. He stepped down on December 13 of that same year.

So we come finally to Angelo Correr, son of the Venetian patrician Nicolò di Pietro, the last pope to leave the throne before Benedict XVI. Elected in 1406, he reigned until 1415 with the name of Gregory XII, then resigned at the request of the Council of Constance in one of the most complex periods of Church history, which was marked by years of battles and disputes that were not just legal but also military and diplomatic. It was necessary to confront the anti-popes Benedict XIII, elected by the faction in Avignon, and John XXIII (whose name would be reused by Angelo Roncalli in October 1958) during the Western Schism. After becoming Angelo Correr again, the ex-pope lived in Recanati, where he died on October 18, 1417.

The topic of resignation came to light again in the past century. Advances in medicine have considerably extended life, and from Pius IX on, the job itself of the successor of Peter has been burdened with responsibilities and functions to the point of making it more and more difficult to carry out for a person who is not fully in possession of physical and intellectual strength. It seems that Pius XI (known in the world as Achille Ratti), who was pope from 1922 to 1939, had already considered the possibility of this step in the final years of his life. It is certain, on the other hand, that his successor, Eugenio Pacelli, Pope Pius XII, did so twice. Elected on the eve of the outbreak of World War II, the Pope came to know about a plan of Adolf Hitler, who wanted to kidnap him and deport him outside of Italy. He informed his close entourage that in the event of a concrete threat of deportation by the Germans, they would "carry off Cardinal Pacelli, and not the pope" as Cardinal Domenico Tardini testified, who at that time was his close collaborator in the Secretariat of State. Pius XII wrote a letter of resignation and had it given for safekeeping to Cardinal Manuel Cereieira Gonçalves, the Patriarch of Lisbon, who had been created cardinal together with Pacelli in the consistory of December 1929. The choice was not accidental: Portugal was a neutral country, not involved in the war. In the event of the deportation of the Pope, the cardinals would be free to gather there and elect a new pontiff. At the end of the war, that document was destroyed.

But Pius XII was also just one step away from resigning several years later, in 1954, when he was struck by illness. However, he recovered, and the idea was abandoned. The idea of resignation occurred also to his successor, Blessed John XXIII. His secretary, Monsignor Loris Capovilla revealed: "Engraved distinctly in my memory is the conversation with Bishop Alfredo Cavagna, confessor and counselor of John XXIII, one Friday in Lent of 1963, in the afternoon, the contents of which I did not immediately commit to writing: His Excellency emerged from the Pope's room after having heard his confession and spoken with him at length about the schemas of the Council. He summoned me to the parlor and without preamble, perhaps supposing that I knew something, told me that the Pope cannot resign.... It is obvious that in the course of the conversation, John XXIII, considering the state of his health and foreseeing the tremendous work involved in conducting the Council, must have declared that he was willing to renounce the papacy."

The possibility was once again under consideration by Paul VI. "He was preoccupied", his confessor, Jesuit Father Dezza, related, "with the thought of a sickness that would render him unable to work, because of the harm to the Church that would result from it". Pope Montini thought seriously, and several times, about the possibility of resigning. He hastened to write a two-page letter, in his own hand, in which he asked the cardinals to convoke the conclave in the event of his prolonged inability and of his incapacity to submit his resignation in a timely fashion. Moreover, Paul VI seriously considered the possibility of leaving the pontificate upon completing his eightieth year—after having set that age limit for cardinals to participate in a conclave. It seems that the decision had already been made, and the mini-consistory of 1977 (in which Cardinal Giovanni Benelli received the purple hat together with Ratzinger) is to be understood in this light. Then, however, he was dissuaded and decided to remain at his post. In recent times, the problem arose with the long and debilitating illness of John Paul II. Blessed Karol Wojtyła talked with his co-workers several times about the possibility of resigning.

The Spanish Cardinal Julian Herranz, a canonist and an Opus Dei priest, revealed that he had been consulted at the end of Wojtyła's pontificate on the question of resignation. And in his book, he reprints the personal note that he himself wrote, on December 17, 2004, "after a conversation" with Archbishop

Stanisław Dziwisz, at that time the Pope's secretary and now Cardinal of Kraków. The passage reads:

> As for the possibility of resignation for reasons of health, I wrote in that note—and now it seems to me opportune to make it known, as an example of the heroic obedience and prudence of John Paul II: "He [Fr. Stanisław] limited himself to commenting that the Pope—who personally is quite detached from the position—lived in abandonment to the will of God. He trusts in Divine Providence. Moreover, he fears creating a dangerous precedent for his successors, because someone could be left exposed to maneuvers and subtle pressures on the part of those who wanted to depose him."

Benedict's resignation, therefore, brings us into uncharted territory. What will he be called? What will he do? Will he go back to being a simple bishop? Canonists of various schools of thought maintain that Ratzinger should be called "former Bishop of Rome" or "former Pope". And even that it would be advisable to set aside the white papal vestments and to put on again his episcopal robes, not the cardinalatial robes, because, with an election to the pontificate, a cleric leaves the College of Cardinals.

But the Vatican spokesman, Father Federico Lombardi, citing Archbishop Gänswein, instead explained Ratzinger's decision: he will be called "Pope Emeritus", will continue to wear a simple white cassock (but without the *mantelletta*, or short cape), and will keep the name "His Holiness Benedict XVI".

On Wednesday, February 27, on a sun-drenched Saint Peter's Square, the Pope, now on the eve of his resignation, held his last General Audience. There was a huge crowd: pilgrims from all parts of Italy and of the world, who had come to embrace the Bishop of Rome who was leaving the papacy to retire to a cloister. The final address of Benedict XVI in Saint Peter's Square is a hymn to hope, to trust in God. Almost a portrait of his successor who two weeks later would appear at the central *loggia*. A text to read and reread attentively, in depth. A "summa" of the thought of Joseph Ratzinger, "the humble worker in the Lord's vineyard".

"I see the Church alive! ... the barque of the Church is not mine but his. Nor does the Lord let it sink; it is He who guides it." A spiritual testament and a lesson for the cardinals who would have to elect the new pope. Serenely and with determination, Benedict XVI, increasingly small and frail, concluded his almost eight-year reign by showing, in spite of everything, the joyous and positive face of a Church of the people. He did not draw up an account, but showed his successor by his example what the pope is and what he must do, through simple catechesis. Light-years away from jockeying for clerical power, from factions, from strategies of ecclesiastical policy studied at one's desk, from the scandals, from the self-referential messages, from the image of a Baroque Church turned inward to contemplate herself. A message that the crowd of pilgrims, who had come to salute him for the last time, understood quite well and listened to with emotion.

In the lesson of Benedict XVI, there was above all gratitude for the reports that he had "heard" from all parts of the world about the faith and charity that "circulate in the Body of the Church". The Pope once again appeared absolutely serene and calm after the decision he had made; in describing his none-too-easy pontificate, he noted: "It has been a portion of the Church's journey which has had its moments of joy and light, but also moments which were not easy." An explicit reference to the travel, to the scandals and the attacks that accompanied those eight years. In order to recount them, Ratzinger recalls the Gospel passage that describes the boat of the apostles at the mercy of the storm: "I have felt like Saint Peter with the Apostles in the boat on the Sea of Galilee: ... there were also moments when the waters were rough and the winds against us, as throughout the Church's history, and the Lord seemed to be sleeping. But I have always known that the Lord is in that boat, and I have always known that the barque of the Church is not mine but his. Nor does the Lord let it sink."

Another image of a boat comes to mind, the one that figured in the last homily of Cardinal Ratzinger, during the opening Mass of the 2005 conclave. Then he spoke about the "little barque" of the thinking of many Christians, shaken by a series of negative "-isms", from atheism to agnosticism. Now, at the moment of his resignation, the pope did not follow the "prophets of gloom". He did not make any pessimistic allusion. Instead, he invited everyone "to entrust ourselves like children in God's arms, certain that those arms always hold us, enabling us to press forward each day, even when the going is rough." Then he added: "I want everyone to feel loved by that God who gave his Son for us and who has shown us his infinite love. I want everyone to feel the joy of being a Christian." A positive, merciful view, therefore.

In his talk, Benedict XVI also included thanks to the cardinals, to his Secretary of State, to his co-workers. He did not want to endorse the interpretation of those who maintained that the undeniable tensions in the Curia were at the root of his resignation. So he told about the letters received from so many "ordinary people", who "do not write to me in the way one writes, for example, to a prince or some important person whom they do not know", but, rather, "as brothers and sisters, as sons and daughters. . . . Here one can sense palpably what the Church is—not

an organization, an association for religious or humanitarian ends, but a living body, a communion of
brothers and sisters." Words that the faithful world-
wide would soon hear repeated on the lips of his
successor, Francis.

In the remarks devoted to his resignation, Benedict XVI stressed that he "asked God insistently",
given the decline in his energies, for light, so as to
make "the right decision, not for my own good,
but for the good of the Church". He explained that
he took this step "with full awareness of its gravity
and also its novelty, but with profound interior serenity". That serenity that, incidentally, shone forth from
his face in those last public appearances. "Loving
the Church", he explained, "means also having the
courage to make difficult, painful decisions, always
looking to the good of the Church and not of
oneself."

Finally, Ratzinger recalled that someone who
becomes pope no longer has any privacy; he "belongs
always and completely to everyone". His resignation did not mean "returning to the private sphere",
going back to doing what he used to do before
becoming pope. It meant remaining "in the service
of prayer", remaining, "in the enclosure of Saint
Peter". "I am not abandoning the cross", he concluded, responding to those who commented on his
decision by comparing it with the different attitude

of John Paul II, who remained on the Throne until the end, "I am ... remaining in a new way at the side of the crucified Lord."

The next morning, a meeting with the cardinals in the Sala Clementina. Among those who paused the longest with the Pope was the Archbishop of Buenos Aires, Jorge Mario Bergoglio. That afternoon, Benedict XVI left the Vatican and, in a helicopter, circling over the Eternal City—an impressive panorama—headed toward the palace in Castel Gandolfo, where he will reside for several months while waiting for workers to finish the remodeling of the cloistered monastery within the Vatican.

3

Padre Bergoglio's Conclave

On Wednesday, February 27, at eight in the morning, by the baggage carousels at International Arrivals of Leonardo Da Vinci Airport (Roma-Fiumicino), three cardinal electors meet. They have just arrived at the same hour on flights coming from Buenos Aires, São Paulo (Brazil), and Manila. They are Jorge Mario Bergoglio, Odilo Pedro Scherer, and Luis Antonio Tagle. The first two are wearing clerical attire. The third is in civilian garb and still looks like a youngster. They know one another. They respect one another. They greet one another. The next day, in the Sala Clementina, when Padre Bergoglio meets Cardinal Tagle dressed in a regulation black cassock with red trimmings, red cape, and *zucchetto*, he tells him jokingly, "You know, yesterday at the airport there was a boy who looked a lot like you ..."

Hummes, Archbishop Emeritus of São Paulo and Prefect Emeritus of the Congregation for the Clergy, would sit right next to Bergoglio in the Sistine Chapel during the conclave. The two have been acquainted for a long time and are friends.

The next day, February 28, at 8:00 in the evening, the Apostolic See becomes vacant. February 28 is a special day in the life of Padre Bergoglio. On exactly that day, fifteen years before, the Archbishop of Buenos Aires, Cardinal Antonio Quarracino, died, and Bergoglio, who was already his coadjutor, succeeded him as the head of the diocese of the Argentine capital. It is impossible that this coincidence of dates could have escaped the Jesuit cardinal. A forewarning?

The future pope is residing as always in the Domus Sacerdotalis Paulus VI, the house for clergy at via della Scrofa 70. He is a regular guest, on the rare occasions when he comes to Rome. Bergoglio is, indeed, a cardinal who does not willingly leave his diocese. On the via della Scrofa they all know him: the staff, the regular guests—priests who meet to concelebrate morning Mass with him. The pre-conclave begins with the General Congregations, the meetings of cardinals who are called together to discuss the future of the Church, her needs, and serious problems.

Bergoglio is accustomed to rising very early in the morning to spend a long time in prayer before the tabernacle. Even on the days leading up to the conclave, he travels on foot, without a *zucchetto* on his head, walking through the alleys in the heart of Rome so as to arrive at the Vatican. The media expectations are high; thousands of journalists from all over the world have arrived in the Eternal City. The cardinals meet in the new Synod Hall, and waiting for them, outside the gates to the square of the Holy Office, are swarms of reporters, photographers, and videographers. They are the gauntlet of the media circus. The television lenses scrutinize the faces of the *papabili*. Padre Bergoglio arrives at a brisk pace, but no one recognizes him. The television news reports these days record his passage several times, without anyone accosting him or asking him questions.

How different the situation is today compared with eight years ago! Then the Archbishop of Buenos Aires, like 113 of the 115 cardinal electors of the successor of John Paul II, was having his first conclave experience. Rome was invaded by pilgrims who had come to pay their respects to the great Pope Wojtyła. The endless crowd that for several days and nights filed past the remains of the Polish pope had somehow influenced the cardinals. It required them to make a rapid choice. And there was someone prearranging matters so as to facilitate the election of Ratzinger. In the Curia, the Colombian Cardinal Alfonso Lopez Trujillo had been the great kingmaker of

Benedict XVI. The conclave had been swift. The cardinals had gathered on the evening of April 18, 2005, and the following afternoon, on the fourth ballot, the pope was elected. Surprisingly, the cardinal with the most votes, after Ratzinger, had been none other than the Archbishop of Buenos Aires. No preparations at all, in his case. A small number of his confreres had already expressed their confidence in him, and that was enough to make many look at him. During the second round of voting in the morning, Bergoglio had come to win a quarter of the paper ballots with his name under the printed inscription, "Eligo in Summum Pontificem". Something happened, however, during the lunch break. The number of electors preferring Ratzinger kept increasing, but the group of Bergoglio supporters had reached the point where, although they could not elect someone, they could block someone.

Then, on the first ballot in the afternoon, the turning point: the Argentine cardinal lost a few votes while continuing to keep a considerable number of them, and Ratzinger was elected. That evening, after the first *Urbi et Orbi* blessing and supper, Cardinal Bergoglio left his room in the Casa Santa Marta and walked toward the Pope's room. He wanted to speak to him, but the Vatican police were already there to guard him, and so he gave up. Maybe that is another reason why, when just elected, on the evening of

March 13, 2013, he wants to continue to share the same table and moments of common life with his "brother cardinals".

If we look at the recent history of the conclaves, we can say that usually the candidate who comes in second in one conclave does not become pope in the next election. Then, too, Padre Bergoglio is already seventy-six years old.

The days preceding Francis' conclave are difficult, marked by attempts to exert pressure and also by the complicated and embarrassing story of the accusations against the Scottish Cardinal Keith O'Brien.

In the days leading up to the *sede vacante*, the retired Archbishop of Los Angeles, Roger Mahony, is the one to end up in the crosshairs. There are groups of victims of pedophiles that clamor for him to be excluded from the conclave: the Cardinal is incapable of dealing with some cases of priests who abused children and youths. Journalists, too, and even Catholic journalists organize polls against the cardinal from the United States, hoping that he will step back or that the Vatican will decide to keep him out of the Sistine Chapel.

There is something disconcerting about the polemics whipped up against Mahony. Failure to act, inadequate reporting, and cover-ups with regard to cases of pedophile priests of his diocese in the eighties and nineties would be a reason—according to his accusers—to prevent him from participating in the vote that will choose the successor of the retired Joseph Ratzinger. But the Apostolic Constitution *Universi Dominici gregis*, promulgated in 1996 by John Paul II, declares: "All the Cardinal electors, convoked for the election of the new Pope by the Cardinal Dean, or by another Cardinal in his name, are required, in virtue of holy obedience, to obey the announcement of convocation and to proceed to the place designated for this purpose, unless they are hindered by sickness or by some other grave impediment, which however must be recognized as such by the College of Cardinals." For a long time, the right of a papal elector to cast his vote without being subject to pressure or conditions has been one of the norms decreed for a conclave.

The idea that there are cardinals unworthy of exercising the most important of the rights connected with their status, and that this "unworthiness" is determined through media polemics, is a dangerous precedent: indeed, there can always be someone who, considering himself purer, will accuse someone else of not being worthy to enter the Sistine Chapel. The Church has always sought—sometimes unsuccessfully—to protect the papal election from outside influences and interference. In 2005 there were protests because of the participation in the conclave by the Archbishop Emeritus of Boston, Bernard Law, who had been forced to resign some years earlier because of his handling of clerical pedophilia cases in his diocese, but the campaigns against his "unacceptability" did not have the same intensity as those against Mahony.

In this specific case, it should also be remembered that the Cardinal Emeritus of Los Angeles made mistakes and underestimated the seriousness of cases of pedophile priests that he dealt with in the past. After John Paul II and Cardinal Ratzinger issued, more than ten years ago, the news norms for addressing these situations, Mahony was one of those who applied them diligently. This is proved by various documents that testify to how he intervened, firmly applying the rules.

Then too, we should not overlook the fact that for decades the approach to these scandals was characterized by a widespread underestimation, even in the Roman Curia. Why should Mahony give up the conclave, while others should not, even though they not so long ago, beyond the Tiber, relied on a different procedural line from the one now adopted? Or those who in Wojtyła's Curia protected the founder of the Legionaries of Christ, Marcial Maciel, a serial abuser, and showed him unconditional respect?

The battle against Cardinal Mahony's participation in the conclave, in the name of political correctness, therefore represents undue pressure that runs the risk of transforming the conclave into a crude copy of a reality show, with a certain number of contestants "nominated" by the public, who vote by text messaging for them to be expelled from the competition.

The Holy See intervenes with a note that is very harsh in its accusations but generic as to its addressees. This is also because Mahony is not the only cardinal who has ended up in the crosshairs: recall the pedophilia scandals in Ireland and Belgium, which would require that Cardinals Danneels and Brady be excluded from the conclave. The Secretariat of State therefore is trying to shield the papal election from international controversies, to which have been added in Italy the poisonous fumes from Vatileaks and the fantastic speculations about the secret report of the three cardinals. The Vatican note rails against the "often unverified, unverifiable, or even completely false news stories that cause serious damage to persons and institutions", with which some seek to influence the cardinals as they enter the conclave.

"Over the course of the centuries," the document recalls, "Cardinals have had to face many forms of pressure, exerted upon individual electors or upon the College of Cardinals itself, that sought to influence their decisions, following a political or worldly logic. Although in the past", the note continues, "the so-called powers, i.e., States, sought to influence the election of the Pope, today there is an attempt to do this through public opinion, which is often based on judgments that do not capture the typically spiritual aspect of this moment that the Church is living." Therefore "it is deplorable that, as we draw closer to the moment when the Conclave will begin and the Cardinal electors will be obliged—in conscience and before God—to express their choice freely, there is a widespread dissemination of often unverified, unverifiable, or even completely false news stories that cause serious damage to persons and institutions." The note concludes: "Now as never before, Catholics are focusing on what is essential: praying for Pope Benedict, praying that the Holy Spirit might enlighten the College of Cardinals, and praying for the future Pope."

In addition to the Vatican note, there is another equally forceful intervention by the spokesman of the Holy See, Father Federico Lombardi, stating that "there are not a few, in fact, who seek to profit from the moment of surprise and disorientation of the spiritually naive to sow confusion and to discredit the Church and her governance, resorting to old devices, such as gossip, misinformation, and sometimes even slander, or exerting unacceptable pressures to influence the exercise of the duty to vote on the part of one or another member of the College of Cardinals whom they consider to be objectionable for one reason or another." The tone here is unusually serious. And fearless, too, is the comparison between the criticism of the ecclesiastical hierarchy by the mass media and the bygone era of interference by kings and emperors in the selection of the successor of Peter.

No sooner do the polemics over the Mahony case begin to calm down than the O'Brien bomb explodes. The Scottish cardinal is accused by some ex-seminarians of having molested them in the eighties. The Cardinal at first vigorously denies but then admits his responsibility: "There have been times that my sexual conduct has fallen below the standards expected of me as a priest, archbishop, and cardinal." O'Brien apologizes "to those I have offended, . . . to the Catholic Church and people of Scotland". Pope Benedict XVI, on the eve of his abdication from the papacy, now accepts the resignation submitted several months earlier by the Archbishop of Edinburgh for reasons of age, but he does not take away his purple hat, symbol of the authority to help elect the new pontiff. O'Brien remains an elector. He himself will be the one to announce publicly his decision not to go to Rome to participate in the conclave. He and the retired Archbishop of Jakarta, who cannot leave Indonesia for health reasons, will be the two absent electors.

In the days immediately preceding the *sede vacante*, Benedict XVI made some last-minute modifications to the rules for the conclave with his Motu Proprio *Normas nonnullas*, dated February 22, 2013, the Feast of the Chair of Saint Peter.

The most significant innovation in the document is found in two lines added to a paragraph of the Apostolic Constitution currently in force concerning the election of a pope: "the College of Cardinals is granted the faculty to move forward the start of the Conclave...." The retiring pope determines, therefore, that the voting to select his successor can begin in the seclusion of the Sistine Chapel several days before the elapse of the fifteen days from the beginning of the *sede vacante* period codified by John Paul II in 1996.

A possible decision to set an earlier date will be made by the congregations of cardinals, which are scheduled to start on Monday, March 4. All the cardinals present in Rome, and thus not only those under eighty years of age who have the right to enter the conclave, can therefore determine an earlier date, provided that all the electors are present and provided that those electors who are prevented from coming to Rome for various reasons have already communicated explicitly their decision not to participate and that their decision has been ratified by the College of Cardinals.

Here is paragraph 37 of the Apostolic Constitution after the revision: "I furthermore decree that, from the moment when the Apostolic See is lawfully vacant, fifteen full days must elapse before the Conclave begins, in order to await those who are absent; nonetheless, the College of Cardinals is granted the faculty to move forward the start of the Conclave if it is clear that all the Cardinal electors are present; they can also defer, for serious reasons, the beginning of the election for a few days more. But when a maximum of twenty days have elapsed from the beginning of the vacancy of the See, all the Cardinal electors present are obliged to proceed to the election."

Benedict XVI does not "advance" the date of the conclave, nor does he suggest that the cardinals do so: he offers them the option of making a decision along these lines, considering also the absolutely unprecedented situation in which the Church is living in this predicament, with the pope resigning and the date of the beginning of the *sede vacante* period known well in advance.

Therefore, nothing substantial is modified in the election formalities. Pope Ratzinger already made a much more important modification several years earlier, when he restored the rule that a two-thirds majority of the cardinal electors is necessary to elect the pope, always and in every case, even after dozens and dozens of inconclusive ballots.

Starting on Monday, March 4, a cold but sunny day, the cardinals meet and begin their discussions.

Many of the speeches are about collegiality and Curia reform. Never before have so many prelates in a pre-conclave called publicly for a change of direction in the management of the Vatican curial "apparatus", which has been disrupted not only by the Vatileaks scandal—the publication of confidential documents purloined from the desk of the Pope's secretary—but also by dysfunction and lack of coordination. Thus the cardinals—speaking one after another in a dialogue that is cordial but frank as never before—address the topic of the organization of the dicasteries, their coordination, their connections with the bishops' conferences. They make suggestions that Pope Francis can ignore only with difficulty. They voice requests that are the result of the experiences—certainly not positive ones—of the last few years in relations between Rome and the local episcopates.

Various cardinalatial heavyweights confront the question without mincing words, either by asking for information about the Vatileaks case or else by speaking about the need for a change of course in the management of the Curia and of the Secretariat of State. The replies to the first request should not be considered exhaustive, because Pope Ratzinger determined that the *Relatio*, or report, on the theft of documents and more generally on certain curial scandals, prepared by Cardinals Herranz, Tomko, and De Giorgi, was to be delivered to his successor. Not to the cardinals before the conclave. Nonetheless, to the cardinal electors who ask for some light on the subject, the three Eminences who conducted the investigation provide some information in one-on-one conversations. Nevertheless, in the hall resound the names of individuals who are presumed to be involved, important lay employees of the Vatican as well as important Italian leaders who in recent years have had the best possible connections with the Secretariat of State. Cardinal Tarcisio Bertone, ex-Secretary of State—who is performing the role of *camerlengo* and therefore is vested with a specific and particular authority during the *sede vacante* period—often ends up the focus of criticism for his managerial style.

As far as the Curia more generally is concerned, whether before or after the presentation of several reform proposals by Cardinal Francesco Coccopalmerio, President of the Pontifical Council for the Interpretation of Legislative Texts, other prelates say they think there should be no more procrastinating about the changes that the now-retired Benedict XVI reportedly mentioned incidentally at the Ash Wednesday ceremony, admitting with regret that he had not succeeded in making them.

There is talk, then, about the need for better communication between the pope and the heads of dicasteries: in other words, access to and a constant exchange with the pontiff. Once there were the

56

so-called "scheduled audiences", predetermined meetings on a calendar that extended a year in advance: not only the prefects of the congregations but also the secretaries, those who were second in command, had access to the pope, so that he could get a firsthand idea of the problems and make decisions. In recent years, the number of "scheduled audiences" had been reduced, the custom remaining only for a few dicastery heads such as the Prefect of the Congregation for Bishops and the Prefect of the former Holy Office. The Secretariat of State increasingly served as a buffer: in recent times, a cardinal who headed a dicastery had to wait several months before being able to meet with the pope.

In the pre-conclave, they talk also about the need for greater coordination and exchange of information within the Curia itself, among the various "offices". The same goes for the relation between the center and the periphery, between the Holy See and the episcopal conferences: it is important that there be more consideration of the needs of the local Churches. It is also important that there be greater collegiality in order to avoid any repetition of the events that have marked the life of the Curia in recent years.

Interventions along these lines, in favor of a different way of running the central government of the Church and suggesting some reforms, are made by the German Walter Kasper, by the Austrian Christoph Schönborn, by the Hungarian Peter Erdö, by the Peruvian Juan Luis Cipriani Thorne, by the Frenchman André Vingt-Trois, by the Spaniard Antonio María Rouco Varela, by the Indian Ivan Dias, by the Slovene Franc Rodé, and by the Italian Giovanni Battista Re. The demands for a change of pace, for more collegiality, for a less isolated papal figure less screened off by the Secretariat of State are destined to carry weight in the conclave.

Another recurring topic in the General Congregations is the management of the IOR, the "Vatican Bank", which was marred in the past year by the still obscure episode of the firing of its president, Ettore Gotti Tedeschi.

It would be a mistake, however, to think that the discussion of the prelates in the General Congregations is focused on the problems of the Curia. There is a sense among the cardinals that the greatest need is for the new evangelization: How to continue on the path initiated by Pope Benedict? How to proclaim the Gospel in a new way to those who have drifted away from the faith in our secularized societies? The Christian mission and proclamation are the topics most often discussed during the debate.

When Cardinal Bergoglio takes the podium on the morning of Thursday, March 7, he gives a speech lasting almost three-and-a-half minutes, thus not using the full five minutes allowed. He speaks about "the joyful proclamation of God's love and mercy", about a Church that comes near to people in the places where they live. It is a striking intervention. Several prelates who listened to his talk comment: "He spoke from the heart." It is in these days of discussion, meetings, lunches and dinners and coffee breaks that the candidacy of the Archbishop of Buenos Aires takes shape. In his case, there are no real kingmakers in the strict sense or campaigns organized in advance. There is instead a widespread and consolidated esteem. Among those thinking of voting for him are the Asian and African cardinals, some South Americans, some from the United States, but even some Italians from the Curia.

Geopolitics matters little in the conclave. Even though Bergoglio is to be the first Latin American pope, his geographical origin is not the essential element that will decide his election. Thus, while practically all the media are holding forth at length about the candidacies of the *papabili*—the Italian Angelo Scola, Archbishop of Milan; the Canadian Marc Ouellet, Prefect of the Congregation for Bishops; the Americans Sean Patrick O'Malley and Timothy Michael Dolan, Archbishops of Boston and New York respectively—various prelates are beginning to think about Bergoglio. The last-mentioned rarely appears in the spotlight directed at the favorites day in and day out by the international media.

After almost a week of meetings, the proposals on the table become more specific and the candidacies consolidate. And yet there is a sense of facing a conclave that is less simple, more complicated than the one eight years ago.

It is Monday, March 11. Scheduled for today is the last General Congregation for the conclave, which will start twenty-four hours later. Padre Bergoglio, in the clergy house on the via della Scrofa, does not celebrate Mass that morning but serves it. That is to say, he acts as an altar server—he, a cardinal—for one of the priests staying there temporarily. A gesture that speaks of his profound humility and recalls what Pope Luciani [John Paul I] decided to do sometimes, asking to serve Mass for his secretary, John Magee. It is 6:30 in the morning. The evening of the following day, that elderly Jesuit bishop who serves Mass for a young priest will hear his own name reecho several times from the ballots being counted under the vaulted roof of the Sistine Chapel.

On Tuesday, March 12, Rome is lashed by wind and rain. In Saint Peter's, Cardinal Angelo Sodano presides at the Mass *pro eligendo Pontifice* (for the election of the Pontiff), which is concelebrated by all the cardinals, both the electors who are under eighty years of age and also the older non-electors who will not be included in the conclave.

Sodano wears the same red chasuble used by Joseph Ratzinger eight years ago. At that time, the Dean of the College, in the Mass before the conclave that was to elect him, spoke in worried tones about the situation of the Church under attack by the world: "How many winds of doctrine we have known in recent decades, how many ideological currents, how many ways of thinking," said Ratzinger, "from Marxism to liberalism, even to libertinism; from collectivism to radical individualism; from atheism to a vague religious mysticism; from agnosticism to syncretism, and so forth." "The mercy of Christ is not a cheap grace; it does not presume a trivialization of evil", the Bavarian cardinal concluded before being elected with an avalanche of votes.

Sodano's homily, in contrast, is a hymn to mercy: the mercy of Jesus "is a love that is especially felt in contact with suffering, injustice, poverty, and all human frailty, both physical and moral". A "mission of mercy" that "has been entrusted by Christ to the pastors of his Church . . . but is especially entrusted to the Bishop of Rome". The skill set described by the elderly Dean of the College, who will not enter into the conclave but still directs the General Congregations, is quite unlike that of a pope-manager who holds a whip over the Curia or that of a rigorist pope who constantly fires off condemnations of secularized society. The Church does not need a sheriff or a delegated administrator. It needs a pastor, a genuine, impassioned witness to the Gospel who gives hope to hearts. The image presented by Sodano is, therefore, the positive image of a pastor dedicated above all to evangelization, to proclaiming Christ, which is "the greatest work of charity" and also "the first and principal contributor to development", as the Cardinal Deacon recalls, citing Pope Ratzinger and the encyclical *Populorum progressio* by Paul VI.

Sodano in his homily speaks about the unity of the Church, about the particular ministry that the pope performs for this purpose, declaring also "that each of us must work to build up the unity of the Church. . . . Each of us is therefore called to cooperate with the Successor of Peter." A possible allusion to the request from many quarters for greater collegiality in running the central government of the Church. Sodano recalls, therefore, that "the higher and more universal the pastoral office, the greater must be the charity of the Shepherd."

The Cardinal, former Secretary of State for Pope Wojtyła and at the beginning of the pontificate of Pope Ratzinger, speaks also about the need for the Holy See to become involved, in the wake of the last few pontiffs, in "initiatives that will be beneficial also for the people and for the international community, tirelessly promoting justice and peace. Let us pray that the future Pope may continue this unceasing work on the world level." A reference to the international role of the Holy See, which in recent years seems to have taken on new dimensions with respect to the major crises in the world.

Sodano concludes the homily by encouraging prayer "that the Lord will grant us a Pontiff who will embrace . . . with a generous heart" the mission of "presiding in charity".

It would be a mistake to draw improper conclusions from the spiritual meditation of the prelate from Asti, but the set of qualifications that emerges from his words seems to suit very well the figure of Bergoglio in particular. Both in the speech of the Archbishop of Buenos Aires to the General Congregations and in Sodano's homily, the key word is in fact "mercy".

At 4:30 that afternoon, the 115 cardinal electors process from the Pauline Chapel into the Sistine Chapel, invoking the Holy Spirit. Directing them, with the duties of a dean, is Giovanni Battista Re. Each one of them swears on the Gospel book to preserve confidentiality concerning the election and, if he is elected, to perform the ministry of Peter. "We likewise promise, pledge, and swear that whichever of us by divine disposition is elected Roman

Pontiff will commit himself faithfully to carrying out the *munus Petrinum* of Pastor of the Universal Church and will not fail to affirm and defend strenuously the spiritual and temporal rights and the liberty of the Holy See."

After the *extra omnes* (everybody out) is pronounced by the pontifical master of ceremonies Guido Marini, the electors listen to a meditation by Cardinal Prosper Grech (who is more than eighty years old and therefore excluded from the conclave) and then decide to take an initial vote immediately.

The first ballot serves as a primary. It allows them to evaluate how many and what sort of candidacies are in play. Jorge Bergoglio is off and running from the start with considerable support; other votes go to Cardinals Angelo Scola, Marc Ouellet, and Odilo Pedro Scherer. The Archbishop of Buenos Aires is therefore not an outsider, a candidate for the second or third day in case of a blocked conclave. Among those voting for him are Asian and African prelates, cardinals from Latin America and the United States, and even a few Italians in the Curia.

We must not forget the speech made by Bergoglio in the hall during the General Congregations or the fact that in recent years, since the 2005 conclave, the authoritativeness of the Argentine cardinal has grown in the external forum. For example, during the work of the 2007 meeting of CELAM

(Latin American Episcopal Conference) in Aparecida and during the Synods of Bishops in which he
has participated.

The "primary" of the conclave, that Tuesday evening, March 12, shows, therefore, the firmness of
his candidacy.

That evening, in the Casa Santa Marta, the cardinals dine, talk, and pray. The night that separates
the first ballot from the second offers an opportunity for meditation so that they can go back to the
Sistine Chapel with clearer ideas. On Wednesday,
March 13, in the morning, the cardinals make haste
to carry out the voting procedures. The smoke at
midday is black. The election at the end of the first
day of the conclave does, however, indicate that "the
Ratzinger effect" has worked for Bergoglio, in other
words, that the Argentine cardinal has gradually won
support, in cascades, without stopping until arriving at the white smoke of Wednesday evening. "The
South American cardinals", said the Brazilian Cardinal Raymundo Damasceno, "greatly appreciated
Bergoglio's worth, therefore clearly many of them
joined in supporting him."

The last ballot of the day is the decisive one. The
Cardinal of Buenos Aires has approached two-thirds
of the votes already in the preceding ballot. While
the votes are being cast, Bergoglio is comforted by
Cardinal Claudio Hummes, his friend, who sits beside

him and will also play a part in the choice of the name of the new pope. At 7:05 P.M.—the hour is recorded by Cardinal Angelo Comastri—the Cardinal of Buenos Aires, having responded "accepto" to the Deacon's question, says to the electors: "Vocabor Franciscus", "I will be called Francis."

The Pope himself would be the one to explain the choice of the name when meeting with journalists on March 16. It is the first time in two thousand years of Church history that a successor of Peter has decided to take the name Francis, and, from the evening of the election on, some have suggested that the *Poverello* of Assisi should not be considered the real inspiration of the choice.

"Some people didn't know why the Bishop of Rome wanted to call himself 'Francis'", says Pope Bergoglio, and so "some thought of Francis Xavier, Francis de Sales ..." Indeed these were recurring interpretations by those who considered it too strange that a Jesuit pope should take the name of the saintly founder of the Franciscans. A decision that did not mature on the basis of an idea but as a result of a comforting embrace of a friend.

"At the election I had the Archbishop Emeritus of São Paulo next to me. He is also Prefect Emeritus of the Congregation for the Clergy, Cardinal Claudio Hummes [O.F.M.]: a dear, dear friend", as the Pope tells the story. "When things were getting a little 'dangerous', he comforted me", he adds, referring to the unstoppable increase of support for his name. "And then, when the votes reached the two-thirds, there was the usual applause because the Pope had been elected. He hugged me and said: 'Do not forget the poor.' " The Pope continues:

> That word stuck here [tapping his forehead]; the poor, the poor. Then, immediately in relation to the poor I thought of Francis of Assisi. Then I thought of the wars, while the voting continued, until all the votes [were cast]. And Francis is the man of peace. And so the name came to my heart: Francis of Assisi. For me he is the man of poverty, the man of peace, the man who loves and safeguards Creation. In this moment when our relationship with Creation is not so good— right? He is the man who gives us this spirit of peace, the poor man ... Oh, how I wish for a Church that is poor and for the poor!

There you have the explanation for the origin of the unprecedented papal name, concluding with a very significant statement. Francis speaks about a Church of the poor and at the same time, from the very start of his pontificate, sends concrete signals along these lines. On this occasion, the Pope does not stop speaking. He goes on to relate humorously to the journalists the words of other cardinals. "Afterward some made various witty remarks. 'But you should have chosen the name Adrian, because

Adrian VI was the reformer, and reform is needed
...' " Indeed, in the preceding days, the cardinals
talked a lot about a possible reform of the Curia.
The Pope obviously does not consider this to be
the priority that defines him.

"And another told me, 'No, no: your name should
be Clement.' But why? 'Clement XV: that way, you
get revenge on Clement XIV, who suppressed the
Society of Jesus!' " That last Clement, who suppressed and dissolved the order in 1773, was a Franciscan pope. An irony of destiny, that the first Jesuit
to become Bishop of Rome should choose the name
of the Little Poor Man of Assisi: he would like, or,
rather, he wants, a poor Church for the poor.

4

Risotto in the Bergoglio House

It was a sultry morning in January 1929. The family of Giovanni Bergoglio arrived in Buenos Aires after a long voyage. Despite the heat and humidity, the grandmother of the father, Rosa Margherita Vasallo, an elegant lady, wore a coat with a fur collar, completely out of place in that temperature. In the lining of the coat was the money from the property that the family had sold. The Bergoglios had left Portacomaro (Portacomé, in Piedmontese), a small town in the province of Asti in Piedmont. They had come there from Castelnuovo, also in Asti, at the beginning of the 1800s.

The negotiations to complete the transaction held up the family longer than expected, so the Bergoglios did not board the *Principessa Mafalda*, which shipwrecked north of Brazil, costing some hundred people their lives. Instead, they departed a few days later, on the *Giulio Cesare*. In Portacomaro, the Bergoglios ran a confectioner's shop. They left everything to emigrate but not really for financial reasons: although economic conditions after the Great War were poor, the Bergoglios had no real need in that regard to leave Italy. They had chosen Argentina above all in order to be reunited with their family: three brothers of the future pope's grandfather were already living in that country on the other side of the world, having made their fortune in South America. A political motive for the decision cannot be excluded, either, as the pope's sister Maria Elena Bergoglio explains: "The situation was difficult, but our family did not lack necessities. I remember my father often repeating that the coming of fascism was really what drove him from Italy."

"Three of my grandfather's brothers had already been there since 1922", Cardinal Bergoglio explained to the journalists Sergio Rubin and Francesca Ambrogetti in the book-length interview *El Jesuita* (published in Argentina in 2010 by Vergara). "They had a paving business in Paraná. They built the large four-story Bergoglio home, which was the first building in the city to have an elevator. . . . There was a brother living on each floor."

Mario Bergoglio, the son of Giovanni and Rosa, father of the future pope, was twenty-one at the time. He was one of the 535,000 Italians who emigrated to Argentina during that decade. But the bonds with relatives back in Portacomaro remained strong. Even as cardinal, Bergoglio stayed in contact with his Piedmontese cousins, sending emails that always contained some Piedmontese expression or other.

"There was the energy of pioneers, and then there were also the so-called migration chains, people traveling with the help of friends and relatives, hoping for some opportunity", explains Professor Fernando J. Devoto, author of *Storia degli italiani in Argentina* (History of Italians in Argentina).

"With the crisis of 1932," the future pope continued, "everything was lost, and they were forced even to sell the family tomb. One of my grandfather's brothers, the president of the business, had already died of cancer, another got things going again and did well, the youngest went to Brazil. My grandfather borrowed 2,000 pesos and bought a store. My father, who was a bookkeeper and worked in the administration of the paving business, helped him by delivering merchandise. Then he got a job with another business. They started over again as naturally as when they came here. I think this shows the strength of our 'race'."

The future pope recounted that at the origin of the move to Argentina was "the very European—and especially very Italian—idea of keeping the family together". Mario Bergoglio married Regina Sivori, an Argentine with Genovese and Piedmontese roots, on December 12, 1935. One year later, December 17, 1936, their first child was born, Jorge Mario. The family lived in the Flores quarter of Buenos Aires, in a small house with burgundy tile. "I think my parents bought it", the sister of the future pope surmises, "because it had an enormous kitchen. After they bought it, they weren't quite sure where to put their five children."

"When I was thirteen months old," the future pope recalled, "my mother gave birth to my brother [Alberto]; there are five of us in all. My grandparents lived very close by, and, to help my mother, my grandmother would come to get me in the mornings; she took me home with her and then brought me back in the evenings. My grandparents spoke Piedmontese with each other, and that's how I learned it. They really loved all of my siblings, but I had the privilege of understanding the language of their memories."

"In my papa," Bergoglio says in the book-length interview, "there was never any trace of nostalgia, he looked ahead. For example, he never spoke to me in Piedmontese. I remember replying to a letter of one of my papa's teachers while I was in the seminary, and I wrote it in my poor Italian. I asked him how to spell a certain word, and I saw his impatience; he answered me brusquely, as if wanting to end the conversation and leave."

The lack of nostalgia, however, did not mean that he had forgotten his origins. "Our father spoke of Italy, of how people lived there, their values. He instilled in us a love for our homeland." But he always spoke in Castillian to his children, Jorge Mario, Alberto Horacio, Oscar Adrián, Marta Regina, and Maria Elena. Of the Bergoglio children, only Maria Elena was able to see her brother step out onto the central *loggia* of Saint Peter's Basilica dressed in white. Not without emotion, the new pope is still able to recite from memory a bit of poetry in Piedmontese, Nino Costa's "Rassa nostrana", which he learned from his grandparents. The poem begins with these words:

> *Drit et sincer, cosa ch'a sun, a smijo:*
> *teste quadre, puls ferm e fidic san*
> *a parlo poc ma a san cosa ch'a diso*
> *bele ch'a marcio adasi, a va luntan.*

> (Straight and sincere, what they are is what they
>   seem:
> obstinate, with firm pulse and healthy liver.
> They say little but know what they are saying;
> although they walk slowly, they travel far.)

According to Pope Bergoglio, Luigi Orsenigo's book *Il grande esodo* (The great exodus) contains important reflections on the drama of Italian immigration.

Did he play with his parents? Jorge Bergoglio nods: "I played *briscola* and other card games with my father. My papa played basketball at the San Lorenzo Club and sometimes took us with him. With Mama, instead, on Saturday afternoons at two o'clock we listened to the operas broadcast by the State radio. Before it began, she would explain the opera to us; she alerted us when the most important and famous aria was about to begin.... The truth is that for me, being with my mama and siblings on Saturday afternoon, getting a taste of art, was something beautiful."

Bergoglio fondly remembers the moments he shared with his family, even cooking. "My mother was paralyzed after she had the last child, the fifth, although she recovered over time. When we got home from school during that time, she would be sitting down peeling potatos, with all of the ingredients ready. She told us how we should mix them together and cook them, for we had no idea what we were doing: 'Now put this in the pot, put that in the pan ...', she would tell us. This is how we learned to cook. We all know how to do it, at the very least *cotolette alla milanese*."

As a bishop, Bergoglio had less time to cook, but "when I lived in the Colégio Máximo, since there was no cook on Sunday, I cooked for my students."

The quality? "Well, I never killed anyone with my food . . ."

The pope's sister Maria Elena explained the family's life together to the Italian newspaper *Reppublica*:

> Before they had me, the youngest, twelve years after Jorge, mother lost another child. And I was thirteen when our father, Mario, died from a heart attack. But until then, it was in 1959, we were a happy family. Above all, we were an Italian family—*Tanos*, they called us in Argentina. I remember the sacredness of Sundays: first we went to Mass, in the church of San José, then the long lunches late into the afternoon. Those never-ending and very beautiful lunches with five, six, even seven courses. And with dessert. We were poor but with great dignity, and always faithful to what was for us the Italian tradition. Mother was an exceptional cook. She made fresh pasta, cappelletti and ragù, risotto piemontese, and delicious baked chicken. She always said that when she married Papa she didn't even know how to make a fried egg. Then our *nonna* Rosa, who fled Piedmont in 1929, taught her the tricks. Grandmother Rosa was a heroine for us, a very brave lady. I'll never forget when she told us how in her town, in Italy, she took the pulpit in church to condemn the dictatorship, Mussolini, fascism.

Francis' sister also spoke of the affinity between the new pope and his father.

> Papa was an accountant, and he was also the only one in the house who had a job. And God knows how hard he worked to raise us. When he came to

Argentina, he already had a degree, but they did not recognize it, and so he worked in a factory. But he could not sign the books; another person did. And because of this, they paid him less than they should have.

He was always a joyful man, and my brother Jorge Mario reminds me so much of him. He never got angry. And he never hit us. That was the big difference between the Italian immigrant families and the other families in Argentina. The man was the authority in the house but without exaggerated masculinity. We—Jorge too, who was the oldest—were terrified of the looks Papa gave us when we knew we were into mischief. For him a look was really enough. Sometimes I would have preferred a hundred lashes to one of his reproachful glances. It annihilated me. He was so in love with Mama, and he always brought her presents. He would take my hand, and we would secretly go out and buy something, anything, for Mama. Jorge always reminded me of both of them: Mama, because he too cooks very well, he makes fantastic stuffed calamari; but above all he reminds me of Papa. On Sunday, Papa did his work at home. He put those enormous accounting books on the table and turned on the phonograph, which filled our little house with music. He listened to opera and sometimes to Italian popular music. Classical music was the soundtrack of our Sundays. Still today, Jorge is like Papa: he loves opera and every so often a good tango. And Edith Piaf. And like Papa, he is the only one of us to be a fan of San Lorenzo.

The Bergoglio family was not well off, nor did they lack the necessities. "We were poor with dignity", the Pope's sister recalls. "At home we didn't throw anything out. Mama succeeded in salvaging some article of clothing for us even from our father's things. A ripped shirt, threadbare pants, were repaired, sewn up, and became ours. Perhaps my brother's and my extreme frugality comes from this. But there was one problem. Mama could never serve the same thing twice in a row for a meal. Papa would be upset. And so she made something up, disguised all the left-overs."

As an adolescent, Jorge played soccer with his friends in the neighborhood. He loved sports. And growing up, he had a passion for the tango as well. When he was twelve, he liked a girl named Amalia, who lived nearby. Today she still lives in the same quarter, surrounded by her children and grandchildren. "He always liked to joke, but he was a gentleman", she says. "Our families, who were Piedmontese immigrants with good principles, thought we were still too young for love." She does not think that her affection for Jorge was anything serious: "Of course not! We were only children, it was something very innocent. We grew up together, but I began to see him more when we turned twelve." Amalia speaks of a sunny and tranquil childhood: "We mostly played on the sidewalk or in the parks in the area. We started to spend all our afternoons together." She says that already at that time the future pope knew something of his vocation. "Once he said to me: 'If you don't marry me, I'm going to be a priest!' So certainly the idea was already floating around in his head, but there were still a few years before he made the decision." In fact, Jorge Bergoglio told a different story about the circumstances that led him to embrace the priesthood and to enter the Society of Jesus.

When he finished primary school, his father told him that along with studies he also needed to find work. "Look, when you start secondary school, you also need to work. I'll look for something for you during vacation." Jorge, who was only thirteen, looked at him, puzzled. Things did not seem to be so tight at home that he needed to find a job. "We didn't have anything extra," the future pope explained in *El Jesuita*, "we didn't have a car or go on summer vacations, but we didn't lack anything." Even if he did not understand the reasons for his request, Jorge obediently followed his father's wishes.

He worked in a sock factory and then would study accounting with the help of his father. During the first two years, he did cleaning. In the third year, he was given some administrative work. The fourth year brought major changes: Jorge began to attend an industrial institute, specializing in food chemistry, working in a laboratory from seven in the morning until one in the afternoon. He had only an hour for lunch before he had to go to his classes at the institute, which lasted until eight in the evening. It was an intense life, tiring, demanding, divided between study and work. And yet the new pope always thanked his father for the decision he had made when he was thirteen.

"I thank my father so much for having sent me to work", said Bergoglio. "Working at a young age was one of the best things that happened to me in life. In particular, in the laboratory where I worked, I learned the good and the evil in every human activity." Bergoglio especially remembers the example of the head of the laboratory, a woman:

> I had an extraordinary boss, Esther Balestrino de Careaga, a Paraguayan who was a communist sympathizer, who, years later, during the dictatorship, endured the abduction of her daughter and a son-in-law and then was abducted with two French nuns, *desaparecidas*, Alice Domon and Léonie Duquer, and assassinated. I loved her very much. I remember that when I brought her an analysis, she said to me: "How quickly you did it!" And immediately after, she asked me: "Did you verify this dosage?" I replied, questioning why I had to, since after all of the preceding dosages this one had to be more or less ... "No, you need to do things right", she scolded me. In other words, she taught me about the seriousness of work. I truly owe much to this great woman.

5

The Confession on September 21

The vocation of Jorge Mario Bergoglio came as a call so clear that it is possible to determine the day and the hour of it. Although in hindsight, as always happens, there are those who are ready to bet that he had always known or foreseen it, we must believe the one directly concerned, who speaks of it as an event that turned his life upside down. Something that burst in unexpected, at a definite moment. A God who comes to seek you before you seek him.

The future pope was seventeen years old and was preparing to celebrate "Student Day", a holiday at the beginning of spring, in the Southern Hemisphere, September 21. At that time, Jorge Mario felt affection for a girl from Catholic Action. "Yes, I was in a group of friends with whom we used to go dancing. Then I discovered my religious vocation",

Bergoglio related in the book-length interview *El Jesuita.*

That September 21, he was preparing to celebrate Student Day with his companions. They had planned a picnic. But the day took a completely different turn. Jorge actually went to his parish church of San José de Flores. There was no particular reason for that visit. And yet a decisive encounter occurred. He found there a priest whom he had never met before and who conveyed to him a deep spirituality. The young man decided to make his confession to him. And during that confession, Jorge Mario "discovered" his religious vocation. He became aware of the fact that he had been called. Something happened that changed his life. To such an extent that he decided not to meet with his friends, who were waiting for him at the railroad station. He went back home instead, because in his heart he had decided to become a priest.

"During that confession something unusual happened to me. I cannot say what, but it was something that changed my life. I would say that it was as though I had been surprised while my guard was down", Bergoglio told the journalists Rubin and Ambrogetti.

It was the surprise, the amazement of an encounter for which I realized I had been waiting. This is the religious experience: the amazement of meeting someone who is expecting you. From that moment on,

God became for me the One who goes ahead of you.
You are seeking Him, and He seeks you first. You
want to meet Him, but He comes to meet you first.

But Bergoglio adds another characteristic that was
destined to become the heart of his ministry as a
priest, a bishop, and now as pope. Indeed, it was
not just "the amazement of an encounter" at the
origin of his religious vocation; it was also the merciful way in which God called him.

The sister of the new pope has related that in
those days Jorge was about to propose to a young
woman. "At that time, it is true, there was a possible engagement; he himself often told me about it,
but without ever telling me the name. It was one of
the girls in his group of friends, the ones at the picnic. On that spring day, September 21, he was supposed to propose to her. But if I keep telling this
story, my brother will end up excommunicating me
. . ." Instead of proposing during the picnic with his
friends, he went to the parish church and understood that his path, or rather the path that Someone
was pointing out to him, was different.

His entrance into the seminary did not occur
immediately after that call. In fact, four more years
would pass. The decision was made but was kept in
his heart, protected, and cultivated. "The matter
ended there for the moment", the protagonist confirms. Jorge continued to work in the testing lab,

completed his studies, and did not yet speak with anyone about his desire to become a priest. "I had a wilderness experience, a 'passive solitude' of the sort that is endured without any apparent reason or because of a crisis or a loss." It was as though this upsetting call, accompanied by the experience of mercy, had needed to mature. "My head was not concentrating on religious questions", he recalled in the book-length interview. "I had a political rest-lessness, which, however, went no farther than the intellectual level. I read *Nuestra palabra y proposito*, a periodical of the Communist Party, and the articles by the most important men of culture enchanted me.... But I never became a Communist."

In the following years, before his entrance into the seminary, Jorge became gravely ill. At the age of twenty-one, he was in danger of dying from a lung infection. At one moment, when his fever spiked, Jorge embraced his mama, desperately asking her, "Tell me what is happening to me!" Regina Maria did not know what to say to him, because the doctors, too, were baffled. He was diagnosed with seri-ous pneumonia, and clinical examinations revealed the presence of three cysts. Once the infection was overcome, and after he had recovered a bit, Jorge had to undergo the removal of the upper part of his right lung. The weeks of convalescence were diffi-cult and the pain tremendous because of the method used then to drain the fluid that had accumulated in the lung.

As young Bergoglio was recovering in the hospital, he was annoyed by the conventional words spoken to him by the friends and relatives who came to visit him: "You will see; you're getting over it now", or else: "How nice it will be when you are able to go back home." There was a pain that he had to confront, an existential anguish that took no consolation from those phrases. Everything changed when a special visitor arrived at his bedside, who forgot about the conventional things to say, the pat phrases. She was a nun, the religious sister who had prepared him for his First Communion.

Her name was Sister Dolores. "She told me something that really struck me and gave me much peace: 'Keep imitating Jesus.'" Lo and behold, in light of those words, even everyday suffering took on a different value. It was not taken away, but it gained significance. "Suffering", Bergoglio explained in the book *El Jesuita*, "is not a virtue in itself, but the way in which it is experienced can be virtuous. We are called to the fullness of happiness, and in this search, suffering is a limit. Therefore you truly understand the meaning of suffering through the suffering of the God-made-man, Jesus Christ."

In this connection, the future pope recalls the dialogue between an agnostic and a believer composed by the novelist Joseph Malègue. The agnostic said that, for him, the problem was: "What if Christ had not been God", whereas, for the believer, it was "What would have happened if God had not become Christ", that is, if God had not become incarnate, had not come to earth to give meaning to our journey. "Therefore," Bergoglio explains, "the key is to consider the Cross as the seed of the Resurrection. Any attempt to alleviate suffering will obtain only partial results unless it is based on transcendence. It is a gift to understand and to experience suffering fully. Moreover, it is a gift to live fully."

Bergoglio maintains that the Church, too, in some moments of her history, has exaggerated the theme of suffering. And he recalls, in this connection, that his favorite film is *Babette's Feast*, released in 1987, written and directed by Gabriel Axel, based on a story with the same title by Karen Blixen.

> Here we see a typical case of the exaggeration of limits and prohibitions. The protagonists are persons who live a Puritan Calvinism, exaggerated to the point where redemption by Christ is experienced as a denial of the things of this world. Then come the freshness of freedom, the squandering of a fortune for a dinner, and they all end up being transformed. This community did not really know what happiness was. Its life was crushed by sorrow. It was tied to a life that had paled. It was afraid of love.

Perhaps for this reason, too, the new pope mentions the *White Crucifixion* by Chagall as a painting he especially likes: "It is not cruel; it is full of hope. It depicts sorrow with serenity. In my judgment, it is one of the most beautiful things Chagall painted." For Bergoglio, "Christian life is giving witness with joy, as Jesus did. Saint Teresa used to say that a sad saint is a sad excuse for a saint."

Returning to the topic of sorrow, the future pope says that what a person who is suffering needs "is to know that there is someone with him, who wishes him well, who respects his silence and prays that God may enter into this space that is sheer solitude."

In Bergoglio's heart, meanwhile, his vocation was maturing. And so, finally, the future pope decided to enter the seminary, and he chose the Jesuits. "I decided on the Society of Jesus because I was attracted by the fact that it was an advance guard of the Church, in which they used military language and were defined by obedience and discipline. I chose it also because the Society was oriented toward missionary ministry. As time went on, I felt a desire to go to the missions in Japan, where the Jesuits have always done very important work. But because of the serious health problem that had stayed with me from my youth, I was not allowed: How many people over there would have been 'saved' by me if they had sent me there?" the future pope recalls with a hint of irony.

Jorge's parents reacted in different ways.

I spoke with my papa and he reacted very well. More than that: he felt happy. He just asked me whether I really felt sure about my decision. Someone said afterward that my mama, like a good mother, had begun to anticipate that I would become a priest. But her reaction, in reality, was different: "I don't know, I don't see you ... You should wait a bit, keep working ... finish at the university ..." The truth is that my dear old mama took it badly. My father understood me more. He had inherited a very strong religious sense from his mother.

The Pope's sister, Maria Elena, interviewed by the Italian daily *La Repubblica*, confirms his account:

When he finished technical school and became a chemical expert, Jorge told my mother that he wanted to study medicine. Then Mama decided to organize the attic overlooking the terrace of our house so that he could study in peace, away from the rest of us. One day, though, she went up there to clean and found only theology books. When my brother came home, she confronted him, asking why he had lied to her. I cannot forget it: "I didn't lie to you, Mama", Jorge answered her calmly. "I did tell you that I wanted to study medicine, but the medicine of the soul." She still took it very badly because she understood that she would soon lose him. Papa, on the other hand, was glad: if it had been up to him, all his sons would have become priests and monks.

His mother's attitude would not change soon. This is how Bergoglio tells the story:

When I entered the seminary, my mama did not travel with me; she did not want to come. For years she did not accept that decision. There were no quarrels between us: it was just that I would go back home to see her, but she did not come to see me at the seminary. And even when she finally accepted my decision, she did so by keeping it at a certain distance. She came to see me in the novitiate in Cordoba and told me that it was a decision that took a lot of time to mature.

But Jorge recalls how his mother, a true believer, knelt down before him at the end of the priestly ordination ceremony to ask for his first blessing.

"A religious vocation", Bergoglio relates in the book-length interview by Rubin and Ambrogetti, "is a call from God to a heart that is waiting for it, consciously or unconsciously. I have always been impressed by the Gospel passage where we read that Jesus looked at Matthew with an attitude that, translated, could be rendered as 'offering him mercy and choosing him'. This is exactly the way I felt God was looking at me during that confession", the confession at the start of his decision to become a priest. "Miserando atque eligendo" is the motto that Bergoglio would select for his episcopal coat of arms. It is also the heart of his message: service for the sake of mercy and the choice of persons based on an offer: "Look, there is someone who wants what is good for you, who calls you by name, who has chosen you. The one thing that is asked of you is that you let yourself be loved."

Don Lorenzo Vecchiarelli, a parish priest at the Church of Saint Timothy in Rome, has been acquainted with the new pope since he was a youth: they used to live together in Buenos Aires and belonged to the same group of friends. In front of the microphones of Vatican Radio, he remembered the time when, during a party, he had seen the young Bergoglio sitting pensively off to the side. He asked him the reason for it. And he answered, "Tomorrow I will enter the seminary!"

"What I remember about him, when we were young", he said, "was his simplicity and a deep seriousness. At one particular time when we met, I felt the impulse of his spirit that desired to enter the seminary. This encouraged me also to enter the seminary: only he joined the Jesuits and I joined the Salesians."

Having entered the seminary in Villa Devoto, Bergoglio then, on March 11, 1958, went to the novitiate of the Society of Jesus. He completed his studies of the humanities in Chile and, in 1963, returned to

Buenos Aires and took a degree in philosophy at the faculty of Saint Joseph Major Seminary in San Miguel. Between 1964 and 1965, he taught literature and psychology at Immacolata College in Santa Fe and in 1966 taught the same subjects at the University of El Salvador in Buenos Aires. He was ordained a priest on December 13, 1969, while studying theology at Saint Joseph Seminary in San Miguel, where he took a degree the following year. After completing his third probation in Alcalá de Henares in Spain, on April 22, 1973, he made his perpetual profession. Now he was a Jesuit priest in all respects.

6

A Priest under the Dictatorship

The *curriculum vitae* of Jorge Mario Bergoglio is somewhat atypical. In the seventies and eighties, the future pope combined academic and teaching activities with parish pastoral ministry and spiritual direction. After a stint as master of novices in 1972–1973 at Villa Varilari, in San Miguel, where he also served as a professor of theology and rector of the major seminary, where, as we mentioned, he used to cook on Sundays for his students, he was elected Provincial of the Jesuits of Argentina, a position he held for six years.

This was the crucial period of the dictatorship of Jorge Rafael Videla Redondo, who was in power in Argentina from 1976 to 1981, after a *coup d'état* that took down Isabelita Perón. His regime was marked by the systematic violation of human rights, including the torture and assassination of thousands of persons. These were the *desaparecidos*, individuals—both men and women—considered opponents of the regime, who, along with their families, were abducted and then killed. The stance taken by Father Provincial Bergoglio with regard to two confreres in those years is at the origin of the false accusations that have been leveled against him. The trumped-up charges had already surfaced like clockwork on the eve of the 2005 conclave, and they were promptly exhumed as soon as Francis appeared at the central balcony of Saint Peter's Basilica.

The source of the accusations is the Argentine journalist Horacio Verbitsky, who, in his books, charges Bergoglio with two serious misdeeds: a decision to dismiss Jesuits Orlando Yorio and Francisco Jalics, since they were hated by the regime because of their work in the *favelas*. And the much more serious crime of having collaborated with the dictatorial regime of Videla. At the time of the incidents, let us remember, Bergoglio was the Provincial of the Jesuits, but he held no ecclesiastical positions of responsibility in the Church in Argentina. And it is not entirely true that, as someone wrote, "as a Jesuit he had enormous power over the ecclesiastical base communities, which did a lot of work in the shanty-towns of Buenos Aires."

The incident was also addressed by the Argentine courts, which by the way are not very partial to the

Catholic Church. Nothing was found against Bergoglio in the course of an investigation into cases concerning children of the *desaparecidos* who had been kidnapped by the military and into the terrible things that took place at the Escuela de Mecanica de la Armada (ESMA, Naval School of Mechanics), a notorious extermination camp for members of the opposition and the headquarters of various "clandestine maternity homes", where at least six thousand people went to their deaths. Verbitsky's accusations were repeated by *Página 12*, a daily newspaper that is now universally considered the official mouthpiece of the president of the Argentine Republic. According to Verbitsky's account, the priests Orlando Yorio and Francisco Jalics supposedly accused Bergoglio of having handed them over to the military. Captured in May 1976, they were detained illegally for five months. During the same campaign, the army also arrested four female catechists and the husbands of two of them. They were never seen again.

Verbitsky was at it again after the election of Pope Francis, claiming that he had found a document in which Father Provincial Bergoglio described his two Jesuit confreres as "subversive". The document has not been produced, and, ironically, it tells against the campaign mounted by the journalist: first of all, because the document dates from a time after the two Jesuits were set free and, in the second place, because there is no evidence that Bergoglio considered the two priests "subversive". Finally, another claim of Verbitsky has been debunked: that the two Jesuits were banished from their Order by a decision of the Provincial. From the document published by Verbitsky we learn in fact that the two Jesuits actually were not expelled from the Society of Jesus, but, rather, they themselves asked to leave. And that Father Jalics' request was denied, because he had already made his solemn profession. Indeed, he has remained a Jesuit.

There is more. It appears quite obvious that the so-called conclusive proof against Bergoglio is nothing more than a tissue of hearsay statements, woven together in the third person by someone in the regime, an underling in the Religious Affairs Office of the Ministry of the Interior. Diversionary tactics and falsifying facts were the daily bread of the Argentine military junta. Further proof that this is an unreliable source is the fact that it is significantly inaccurate about internal procedures of the Society of Jesus.

"In summary," notes Professor Matteo Luigi Napolitano, a historian who has studied the dossier of the case, "the document published by *Página12* is not a document by Bergoglio, does not reflect his thought, and can legitimately be considered a document 'of the regime' made for the use and consumption of the dictatorial authority so as to control the opposition and to give the impression that somehow it had the support of the Argentine Church."

There are also others who have maintained that Verbitsky's anti-Bergoglio interpretation is misleading, among them Jorge Ithurburu, President of the March 24 Association, an organization that has acted as plaintiff in lawsuits brought against Argentine military men. In an interview granted to the Italian daily newspaper *Il Sole 24Ore*, Ithurburu rejected the accusations against the new pope concerning his relations with the dictatorship. "The responsibility of the Catholic Church as an organization is one thing, and the responsibility of individuals is another. Bergoglio at that time was not even a bishop, and there is no sign of his individual responsibility [in the matter]."

Why, then, did the Provincial, Father Jorge, ask the two Jesuits involved in the base communities to cease their work in the *favelas*, a request they refused? Evidently, Professor Napolitano writes, "he foresaw what would happen, since with the accession of the dictatorship the two Jesuits were abducted and incarcerated at ESMA (the Naval School of Mechanics, in other words, the academy for naval officers, which became a place of detention and torture). The two Jesuits would be released from the ESMA after around six months."

Ithurburu himself notes: "It is obvious that the episode can be interpreted in two ways: the superiors of the two Jesuits are responsible for having left them in the lurch, or else one can think that the same superiors intervened to have them set free. I would lean toward the second hypothesis: the ESMA set no one free by chance, but no one in the Church will ever admit that secret negotiations were conducted. The Church does not speak about these things. The liberation of the two priests, however, remains a fact."

On March 15, 2013, the Vatican spokesman, too, Father Federico Lombardi, branded as "slanderous and defamatory" the campaigns against the Pope, noting their "anti-clerical cast". Indeed, Lombardi added that, in regard to Bergoglio, "this was never a concrete or credible accusation. . . . He was questioned by an Argentine court as someone aware of the situation but never as a defendant. He has, in documented form, denied the accusations. Instead, there have been many declarations demonstrating how much Bergoglio did to protect many persons at the time of the military dictatorship." Well known also is "Bergoglio's role, once he became bishop, in promoting a request for forgiveness of the Church in Argentina for not having done enough at the time of the dictatorship".

A secret document preserved in Washington about those years of Argentine tyranny in a way, albeit indirectly, corroborates the words of the Vatican spokesman. "This document", Napolitano writes, reports verbatim (in the original Spanish) the declarations of General Videla himself, the instigator of the military coup. Videla, after seizing power, observed that "the present situation in the Country is misgovernment, administrative chaos, venality, but also the existence of currents of public opinion and of political convictions that are deeply rooted, with a working class outside the prevailing current ... with a Catholic Church alarmed by the process yet still determined to denounce any abuse against human dignity" (Defense Intelligence Agency, *Forwarding of Spanish Documents*, March 25, 1976: Philosophy and Bio of LTGEN Jorge Rafael Videla, March 24, 1976, p. 1, 10 USC 424, National Security Archive).

An Argentine Church that, as Videla puts it, was "still determined to denounce any abuse against human dignity" is not exactly the picture described by Horacio Verbitsky. This certainly is not to say that there was no collusion or underestimation of the rampant injustices, but the reality is more complex than what is described in the anti-Bergoglio dossiers made available to the international press a few minutes after the election. Nor can we rule out the possibility that this material, as often happens on the occasion of a papal election, could have been delivered by someone who was associated also with some of the cardinals. On the other hand, nothing came of it.

The charges are ultimately contradicted by the direct testimony of Father Jalics: one of the two Jesuits involved, whom Bergoglio supposedly had "dismissed" from the Society of Jesus. In an article posted on the website of the German Province of the Jesuits, Father Jalics felt the need to make some clarifications. It is worth reading them.

> Beginning in 1957 I lived in Buenos Aires. In 1974, prompted by an inner desire to live the Gospel and to call attention to the terrible poverty, and with the permission of Archbishop Aramburu and then-Provincial Father Jorge Mario Bergoglio, I moved with a confrere into a *favela*, one of the poorest districts in the city. While living there, we continued teaching at the University.
>
> The situation in Argentina at that time resembled a civil war. During that period, and more precisely within the space of two years, approximately 30,000 people, leftist guerillas and also innocent civilians, were assassinated by the military junta.
>
> The two of us living in the slum never had contact either with the junta or with the guerillas. Nevertheless, due to the lack of information at that time and also because of deliberate disinformation, our position was misunderstood even within the Church. At that time, we lost contact with one of our lay co-workers, when this person joined the guerillas. Nine months later, after he had been captured and interrogated by the soldiers of the junta, they heard that he was in contact with us.
>
> Assuming that we, too, had something to do with the guerillas, we were arrested. After a five-day hearing, the officer who had conducted the interrogation

told us in these words that he would let us go: "*Padres*, you are not guilty at all. I will make sure that you can return to the poor district." Despite this assurance, we were then, in a way that seemed inexplicable to us, detained for five months, blindfolded and hand-cuffed. I cannot take any position about the role of Father Bergoglio in this situation we experienced. After our release I left Argentina.

Only years later did we have an opportunity to dis-cuss what had happened with Father Bergoglio, who meanwhile had been appointed Archbishop of Bue-nos Aires. Afterward we celebrated a public Mass together and solemnly embraced each other. I am rec-onciled with those events and regard them as finished as far as I am concerned.

I wish Pope Francis God's abundant blessing on his ministry.

Father Franz Jalics, S.J.

How did the future pope respond to the thirty-three questions of the Argentine judges in April 2011? The document was published by the Italian daily newspaper *Avvenire*: "I did what I could, what was possible for me given my age [he was less than forty years old] and the few contacts I had, in order to intercede to have illegally detained persons set free", Bergoglio had reported. This reconstruction of the situation is confirmed by the results of the investi-gation, which never considered him under investi-gation, unlike other priests who were questioned and then charged with crimes.

German Castelli, one of the three judges who wrote the sentence in the trial against the military officers of the ESMA, explained to the daily newspaper that the accusations against the man who is now Pope Francis "were carefully examined by us. We verified all the facts and unanimously concluded that Bergoglio's conduct had no judicial relevance."

Indeed, as the then-Cardinal of Buenos Aires had declared two years before, "I saw General Jorge Videla and Admiral Emilio Massero twice." To his detractors, those meetings appeared to be proof of Bergoglio's collaboration. In reality, the future pope wanted to "find out which military chaplain was celebrating Mass" in the torture centers. Once he learned the name directly from Videla, Bergoglio cleverly convinced the priest-soldier "to pretend to be sick and to send me to his post". This is proof that the Jesuit did not trust some men of the Church and that he had decided to risk it alone. A decision consistent with his advice to "a young man who resembled me a lot" to flee the country. "I gave him my identification and clerical garb; that was the only way that I could save his life."

Bergoglio personally asked Videla about the fate of the arrested priests. "To say that Jorge Bergoglio handed over those priests is absolutely false", Judge Castelli repeated. The future pope had confided to a friend "that he worked like crazy" in the five months in which his Jesuit confreres were held prisoner. "I was never in the places of detention, except once," Bergoglio related to the judges, "when I went together with others to an air force base near San Miguel, in the city of José C. Paz, to ascertain the fate of one *muchacho*."

The accusations trotted out for political purposes in the days after the election of Pope Francis, like the written report about him containing these same accusations that was allegedly circulated among some cardinals, "are a dirty trick", to use the expression of Julio Strassera, a historian and attorney in the trial against the military junta that was responsible for the dark years of the *desaparecidos*. "All of it is absolutely false", Strassera says. The Argentine judiciary system, as organizations like Amnesty International confirm, is considered the most advanced in Latin America. They have never been known to make allowances for the Church, as proved by the case of Father Christian von Wernich, who was a police chaplain sentenced six years ago for his role in seven homicides, forty-two abductions, and thirty-one counts of torture.

Among Bergoglio's chief "accusers" are several ex-guerillas, *montoneros*. "Knowing that the path of violence had led to the coup, they followed it ruthlessly", declares Loris Zanatta, instructor of Latin American History at the University of Bologna, in one of his books recently published by Laterza. "Once the military had seized power," the scholar writes, "they thought the people would rebel. A populace that was in reality exasperated by years of violence and ideology, which did not change with the ascent of Videla."

One of the leaders of the *montoneros* guerillas was, of all people, Horacio Verbitsky. Oddly enough, after Cardinal Bergoglio spoke out in 2005 against President Nestor Kirchner—to whom the Argentine journalist was particularly close—lo and behold, Verbitsky published a book with a chapter attacking the Archbishop of Buenos Aires. The cardinal whom Kirchner had described as "the real head of the opposition".

Finally, it is worth recalling that a winner of the Nobel Peace Prize, Adolfo Pérez Esquivel, a fierce opponent of the military, promptly came to Bergoglio's defense, declaring in a BBC interview that Bergoglio "had no ties with the Argentine dictatorship. There were bishops guilty of complicity with the dictatorship, but not Bergoglio. He is called into question because they say that he did not do what was necessary to get two priests out of prison while he was superior of the Jesuits. I know for certain that many bishops asked the junta to set priests free, and it was never granted."

Further confirmation is provided by the letter that the then-Provincial of the Jesuits sent in 1976 to the brother of Francisco Jalics, one of the two abducted priests. The letter was quoted in March 2013 by the *Frankfurter Allgemeine Zeitung*: "I have made many attempts to persuade the government to set your brother free. Until now I have had no success, but I have not lost hope that he will soon be released." The Provincial wishes him well and says, "I will do all that I can to have him freed.... I have made this matter MY matter; the misunderstandings that your brother and I had concerning religious life have nothing to do with it."

Concerning these accusations, the Pope's sister, Maria Elena, said in an interview with the Italian daily newspaper *La Stampa*: "Does it seem possible to you? It would mean betraying the lesson that our faith had taught us by his difficult choice of life. My brother protected and helped many people who were persecuted by the dictatorship. Those were dark times, and he acted prudently, but his commitment to the victims has been proved."

Later on, as Archbishop of Buenos Aires, the future pope, together with the other Argentine bishops, would compose a request for forgiveness for the attitude adopted by ecclesiastics during the dictatorship.

Because at various moments in our history we were tolerant of totalitarian positions that violate the democratic freedoms that flow from human dignity. Because through our actions and omissions we discriminated

against many of our brethren, without becoming suf-
ficiently involved in defending their rights. We beg
God, the Lord of history, to accept our repentance
and to heal the wounds of our people.

O Father, we have the duty to remember in your
presence these tragic, cruel acts. We ask forgiveness
for the silence of those in positions of responsibility
and for the actual participation of many of your children in that political conflict, in violence against freedom, in torture and in espionage, in political
persecution and in ideological intransigence, in con-
flicts and in wars, in the senseless death that bloodied
our Country. O good and loving Father, forgive us
and grant us the grace to forge again our social ties
and to heal the still-open wounds in your community.

7

A Cardinal on the Subway

How does someone experience prayer who as a youth, on that long-ago September 21, during a confession in a parish church, felt that he was surrounded by an embrace of mercy and chosen for the priestly life?

"For me, praying is in a certain way an experience of trust", Bergoglio explains in the book-length interview *El Jesuita,*

in which our whole being is in the presence of God. This is where dialogue, listening, and transformation occur. Looking at God, but above all sensing that we are being watched by Him. This happens, in my case, when I recite the Rosary or the psalms or when I celebrate the Eucharist. However, I would say that I have this religious experience whenever I start to pray for an extended time in front of the tabernacle. Sometimes I doze while remaining seated and just let Him look at me. I have the sense of being in someone else's hands, as though God were taking me by the hand. I believe that it is important to arrive at the transcendent otherness of the Lord, who is the Lord of all yet always respects our freedom.

Jorge Mario Bergoglio continues to consider himself as being the first in need of the mercy that he preaches and to which he witnesses.

The truth is that I am a sinner whom the mercy of God called in a special way. From my youth, life has entrusted to me tasks of governing—I had just been ordained a priest when I was appointed master of novices and, two and a half years later, Provincial—and I had to learn as I went along, starting with my mistakes, because I made some. Mistakes and sins. I would be a hypocrite if I said that nowadays I ask forgiveness for the sins and offenses that I might have committed. Today I ask forgiveness for the sins and offenses that I have actually committed.

"What grieves me more", Bergoglio also tells the journalists Rubin and Ambrogetti, authors of the book-length interview, "is many times not having been understanding and impartial. In my morning prayer, at the moment of the petitions, I ask to be understanding and impartial, and then I continue by asking for a lot of other things that have to do with the defections along my journey."

The new pope taught for a long time. In his style of instruction, the encounter with the person is an essential element. In the book *El Jesuita*, Bergoglio offers an example of this approach.

> I remember that in the early nineties, while I was an assistant priest in Flores, a girl from a secondary school in Villa Soldati, who was in her fourth or fifth year of the program, got pregnant. It was one of the first instances at that school. There were various opinions about how to address the situation; some were even considering the girl's expulsion, but no one asked or cared about what she was going through. She was afraid of the reactions and allowed no one to get close to her. Until a young instructor, a husband and father, a man whom I greatly respect, offered to speak to her and to look for a solution together with her. When he saw her during a recess, he gave her a kiss, took her hand, and asked her gently: "So you are becoming a mother?" The girl started to cry and did not stop. This gesture of nearness helped her to open up and tell about what had happened to her. And it allowed her to arrive at a mature, responsible answer to her dilemma, so that she avoided missing years of school and remaining alone to confront life with a child. But she also avoided—because this was the danger—being considered a heroine by her classmates for having become pregnant.
>
> What the instructor did was to bear witness to her by going to meet her. He ran the risk of hearing the girl reply, "And what does it matter to you?" But for his part, he was very compassionate, and the fact that he approached her showed that he wished her well. When you try to educate only with theoretical

principles, while overlooking the fact that the important thing is who we have in front of us, you fall into a sort of fundamentalism that is of no use to young people, because they do not assimilate the lesson of being accompanied by a close, living witness.

From this insight, Bergoglio derives also a bit of advice for confessors. He asks them, when they go into the confessional, to be neither rigorists nor laxists. "The rigorist is someone who applies the norm and nothing else: the law is the law, period. *Basta*." The laxist "sets it aside: it is not important, nothing will happen ... just go on that way." The problem, explains the future pope, "is that neither one cares about the person in front of him". And so, what should confessors do? "Be merciful."

Anyone acquainted with Padre Bergoglio knows how important the personal relationship is for him, the personal encounter, attention to the person. One of his anecdotes helps us to understand this better. As Auxiliary Bishop of Buenos Aires, he had to travel one day to conduct a series of spiritual exercises in a convent outside the city, and he had to take the train. As the hour drew near, he left his office in the archbishop's chancery to go pray for a few minutes in the cathedral. As he was leaving, a young man who appeared to be psychologically disturbed approached to ask him whether he could hear his confession. The young man spoke as though he were

drunk, probably under the influence of some drug.
"I, the witness to the Gospel, who was engaged in
the apostolate, told him: 'Soon a priest will arrive,
and you can confess to him, because I have to do
something else.'" Bergoglio knew that that priest
would arrive a short time later. "I walked away,
but after a few steps, I felt tremendous shame. I
retraced my steps and told the young man, 'The
priest is going to be late; I will hear your confession.' After hearing his confession, I brought him
to Our Lady to ask her to protect him. Finally I
went to the station, thinking I had missed the train.
When I arrived, I realized there had been a delay
and, so, I managed to take the train as planned. On
the way back, I did not go home directly, but first
went to my confessor, because what I had done
weighed on me: 'If I do not confess, tomorrow I
cannot celebrate Mass ...'"

For Bergoglio, the delayed train had been a "sign
from the Lord that told me: 'You see that I am directing the story.' How often in life it is better to slow
down and not try to settle everything at once!" It is
necessary to have patience, not to claim to have a
solution for everything, and to "put into perspective the mystique of efficiency".

In March 1986, Padre Bergoglio traveled to Germany, to Munich in Bavaria, to complete his doc-
toral thesis. When he returned, his superiors assigned

him to the University of El Salvador and then to
the church of the Society of Jesus in Cordoba, as
spiritual director and confessor. He heard confes-
sions a lot and continued to do so even as a bishop.
His appointment as Auxiliary of Buenos Aires came
a few years later.

It was May 13, 1992. Padre Bergoglio had a good
rapport with the apostolic nuncio in Argentina, Archbishop Ubaldo Calabresi. He would keep in touch
with the prelate's family, even after Calebresi's death,
and during every trip to Rome he would always
set aside time for a dinner or a lunch with the
nuncio's sister. Calabresi consulted Bergoglio regu-
larly to ask information about priests who were candidates for the episcopacy. That day, however, he
called to tell him that this time the consultation
would have to take place in person. Since the air-
line ran the flight from Buenos Aires to Cordoba
to Mendoza and then back, Calabresi "asked me to
be at the airport [in Cordoba] while the plane went
on to and then returned from Mendoza. So it was
that we talked there—it was May 13—he consulted me on various questions, and when the plane
that had already returned from Mendoza was about
to leave on the return flight to Buenos Aires and
they had called for the passengers to board, he
informed me: 'Ah ... one last thing... You have
been appointed the Auxiliary Bishop of Buenos

Aires, and the appointment will be announced on the 20th ...' That is how he told me."

Bergoglio froze and stood there petrified. As he always does following a stroke of fortune, whether good or bad. So he began his episcopal ministry as the Auxiliary Bishop of Cardinal Antonio Quarracino. In no way did he change his style, his approach to persons, the simplicity of his way of life, his avoidance of worldly occasions.

In the book-length interview *El Jesuita*, he also tells the story of how, five years later, he was appointed Coadjutor Bishop of Buenos Aires, a promotion from Auxiliary to the designated successor of the Cardinal, who was seriously ill.

> I was Vicar General of Cardinal Quarracino, and when he asked Rome for a Coadjutor Bishop, I in turn requested that he not send me to another diocese, but allow me to act instead as auxiliary of a vicariate in the vicinity of Buenos Aires.... But on May 27, 1997, in midmorning, the nuncio Calabresi called me and invited me to lunch. When we were having coffee and I was about to thank him and leave, I saw that they were bringing in a cake and a bottle of champagne. I thought that it was his birthday and was about to congratulate him.... "No, it is not my birthday", he replied with a broad smile. "What is happening is that you are the new Coadjutor Bishop of Buenos Aires."

By the time when he went from being Coadjutor Bishop to Archbishop, the successor of Quarracino, who died on February 28, 1998, Bergoglio could already count on the growing esteem of the clergy of the city, especially of the younger clerics. All the priests of Buenos Aires appreciated his kindness, his simplicity, his wise counsel. None of that would change once he became the Shepherd of the Archdiocese. He installed a direct telephone so that his priests could call him at any hour of the day if they had a problem. There must not be any barriers, secretaries, filters. The bishop was available for his clergy at any moment.

Bergoglio continued to spend nights in the parish, he personally assisted the sick priests, spending hours in the hospital at their bedside. At first he refused to go live in the elegant archbishop's residence in Olivos, staying in a smaller apartment. Then he took only a modest bedroom in the palace. He still liked to cook for his guests. Washing dishes was no problem for him. He welcomed to his house a former auxiliary bishop who needed assistance and looked after him.

He continued to respond personally to all telephone calls, to arrange personally his own schedule of appointments. He did not have a private secretary, but employed various co-workers and a few nuns. He continued to travel by bus—which he preferred because from a bus you could see the people along the street—or by subway. The inhabitants of the Argentine capital learned to recognize him and got to know him. He dressed simply. When he traveled, Jorge Mario—who likes to be described as "a priest who is happy to be a priest"—was inseparable from his date book, in which were written by hand the telephone numbers of his friends and acquaintances. And he always carried with him his Breviary, in which he preserves a letter and the testament of his grandmother, which were written before his priestly ordination, in case she died before the ceremony took place. "I am very attached to the Breviary", he explained in the book-length interview *El Jesuita*. "It is the first thing I open in the morning and the last thing I close before going sleep." Found among those pages is also the text of "Rassa nostrana", a poem in the Piedmontese dialect by Nino Costa.

At the request of the journalists Rubin and Ambrogetti, who were interviewing him, Bergoglio had opened the Breviary, taking out the letter from his grandmother for his ordination and reading it: "On this beautiful day on which you can hold in your consecrated hand Christ our Savior and on which a broad path for a deeper apostolate is opening up before you, I leave you this modest gift, which has very little material value but very great spiritual value." Together with this letter, the grandmother, who nevertheless was able to attend the ordination of Padre

113

Jorge, wrote also a little will and testament, which reads: "May these, my grandchildren, to whom I gave the best of my heart, have a long, happy life, but if someday sorrow, sickness, or the loss of a beloved person should fill them with distress, let them remember that a sigh directed toward the tabernacle, where the greatest and noblest martyr is, and a look at Mary at the foot of the Cross can make a drop of balm fall on the deepest and most painful wounds."

In 2001 John Paul II created him cardinal. It was the largest consistory for new cardinals in the history of the Church. Concerning his thriftiness, the story is told that after the announcement that he had been created cardinal, he did not want to buy the red clothes, preferring to have alterations done to the ones left by his predecessor. On that occasion, Archbishop Bergoglio asked his fellow Argentines who wanted to accompany him to Rome not to do so and, instead, to donate the cost of the trip instead for the needs of the poor. He would do the same after his papal election.

The cardinalate was for him an opportunity to return to his Piedmontese origins. "Yes, when he was appointed cardinal," his sister Maria Elena recalls, "we went to Turin and then to Portacomaro, the region from which my father had come. I admit that it was very moving. The site is magnificent; we went together on a tour of the nearby hills. But to see the house where my father was born, the garden in which he played as a child, the cellar where our uncle made wine: indescribable, an emotion that cannot be communicated in words."

Bergoglio's Church is open and missionary. Interviewed in 2007 by Stefania Falasca for the monthly magazine *30Giorni*, the future pope explained:

> I didn't say that pastoral systems are useless. On the contrary. In itself, everything that leads by the paths of God is good. I have told my priests: "Do everything you should, know your duties as ministers, assume your responsibilities, and then leave the door open." Our sociologists of religion tell us that the influence of a parish has a radius of six hundred meters. In Buenos Aires there are about two thousand meters between one parish and the next. So I then told the priests: "If you can, rent a garage, and, if you find some willing layman, let him go there! Let him be with those people a bit, do a little catechesis, and even give Communion if they ask him." A parish priest said to me: "But Father, if we do this, the people then won't come to church." "But why?" I asked him: "Do they come to Mass now?" "No", he answered. And so! Coming out of oneself means also coming out of the fenced garden of one's own supposedly unchangeable convictions, if they risk becoming an obstacle, if they close off the perspective that is God's. And this applies to the laity.

The new pope considers it a mistake to clericalize the laity:

115

The priests clericalize the laity and the laity beg us to be clericalized.... It really is sinful complicity. And to think that baptism alone would suffice. I'm thinking of those Christian communities in Japan that remained without priests for more than two hundred years. When the missionaries returned, they found them all baptized, all validly married in the eyes of the Church, and all their dead had had a Catholic funeral. The faith had remained intact through the gifts of grace that had gladdened the lives of these laypeople, who had received only baptism and had also lived out their apostolic mission by virtue of baptism alone. One must not be afraid of depending only on His tenderness.

In connection with this, in that same interview with *30Giorni*, Bergoglio recalled the biblical story of the prophet Jonah.

Jonah had everything clear. He had clear ideas about God, very clear ideas about good and evil. About what God does and about what He wants, about who was faithful to the Covenant and who, instead, was outside the Covenant. He had the formula for being a good prophet. God broke into his life like a torrent. He sent him to Nineveh. Nineveh was the symbol of all the separated, the lost, of all the marginalized of mankind. Of all who are excluded and estranged. Jonah saw that the task entrusted to him was only to tell all those people that the arms of God were still open, that the patience of God was there and waiting, to heal them with His forgiveness and nourish them with His tenderness. Only for that reason had God sent

116

him. He sends him to Nineveh, but instead Jonah runs off in the opposite direction, toward Tarshish.

"Running away perhaps from a difficult mission?" the interviewer, Stefania Falasca, asks. "No", Bergoglio replies.

What he was fleeing was not so much Nineveh as the boundless love of God for those people. That was what did not fit into his plans. God had come once ... "and I'll see to the rest." So Jonah had told himself. He wanted to do things his way, he wanted to control it all. His stubbornness confined him within his own structures of evaluation, his ready-made methods, his correct opinions. He had fenced off his soul with the barbed wire of those certainties which, instead of giving freedom with God and opening horizons of greater service to others, had ended up deafening his heart. How the isolated conscience hardens the heart! Jonah no longer knew how God was leading his people with the heart of a Father. . . .

Our certainties can become a wall, a jail that imprisons the Holy Spirit. Someone who isolates his conscience from the journey of the people of God does not know the joy of the Holy Spirit that sustains hope. That is the risk run by the isolated conscience. Of those who from the closed world of their Tarshish complain about everything or, feeling their own identity threatened, rush into battles, only to be still more self-concerned and self-referential in the end.

In Buenos Aires, Bergoglio was a popular archbishop, in the sense of being genuinely close to the people. As demonstrated by his Masses celebrated in the populous *barrios* of the Argentine capital. In August 2008, on the feast of Saint Cajetan, the future pope had a dialogue with the people during his homily:

"I will ask you a question: Is the Church a place that is open only to the good?"

"Nooo!"

"Is there room for the wicked, also?"

"*Siiiii!!!*"

"Do we chase someone away here because he is bad? No, on the contrary, we welcome him with more affection. And who taught us this? Jesus taught us this. Imagine, then, how patient the heart of God is with each one of us."

Examples of this "Church of the people" desired by Bergoglio, the Church that "facilitates" the faith of individuals instead of "regulating it", are contained in another interview that the Cardinal granted in [August] 2009 to his friend, the journalist Gianni Valente, published in *30Giorni*.

Just a few days ago, I baptized seven children of a woman on her own, a poor widow, who works as a maid, and she had had them from two different men. I met her last year at the Feast of San Cayetano [Cajetan]. She had told me: "Father, I'm in mortal sin, I have seven children, and I've never had them baptized." It had happened because she had no money to bring the godparents from a distance or to pay for the party, because she always had to work.... I suggested that we meet to talk about it. We spoke on the phone, she came to see me, told me that she could never find all the godparents and get them together ... In the end I said: let's do everything with only two godparents, representing the others. They all came here, and after a little catechesis I baptized them in the chapel of the archbishop's chancery. After the ceremony, we had a little refreshment. A Coca-Cola and sandwiches. She told me: "Father, I can't believe it, you make me feel important...." I replied, "But *Señora*, where do I come in? Jesus is the one who makes you important."

Bergoglio believes it is necessary to remember the fundamental criterion expressed in the last canon of the Code of Canon Law: The supreme law is the salvation of souls. As a bishop, he said that what caused him the most sorrow was to learn that some priests refused baptism to the children of couples who were not validly married, who were born outside of the "sanctity of marriage".

The child has no responsibility for the marital state of his parents. And then, the baptism of children often becomes a new beginning for parents. Usually there is a little catechesis before baptism, about an hour, then a mystagogic catechesis during the liturgy. Then, the priests and laity go to visit these families to continue with their post-baptismal pastoral care. And it often happens that parents who were not married in church maybe ask to come before the altar to celebrate the sacrament of marriage.

Bergoglio hopes that a tradition found in the most remote areas of Argentina, in those towns and villages where the priest manages to visit only a few times a year, will not die out.

> But there, popular piety feels that children should be baptized as soon as possible, and so in those places there is always a layman or laywoman known by everyone as *bautizadores*, who baptize the children when they are born, awaiting the arrival of the priest. When the priest comes, they bring him the children so he can anoint them with holy oil, completing the ceremony.

Citing the final document, which Bergoglio played a major role in drafting, of the Aparecida Conference, the great meeting of the Latin American episcopate held in May 2007 in Brazil, the future pope invites Catholics to be missionaries.

> The Conference . . . in Aparecida reminded us to proclaim the Gospel by going out to find people, not by sitting [around] waiting for people to come to us. . . . Apostolic zeal . . . is expressed not so much by planning exceptional initiatives or events. . . . It is in ordinary life that missionary work is done. And baptism is paradigmatic in that regard. . . . The sacraments are for the life of men and women as they are. Who maybe don't talk much, but their *sensus fidei* grasps the reality of the sacraments with more clarity than that of many specialists.

For Bergoglio, the Church cannot be made up of an elite. And there can be no pure, minority Church as opposed to that of the masses, populated by that large number of persons for whom Christianity is made up of a few elementary things, a few practical essentials. The new pope does not agree with the rigorists who refuse baptism and the other sacraments to those who request them but are considered unsuitable because they are not practicing their faith.

This is why he says that priests need "to look at our people, not as they ought to be, but as they are and to see what is necessary. Without preconceived ideas and prescriptions but with generous openness. Through His wounds and frailties, God spoke. Let the Lord speak.... In a world that we will not succeed in interesting with the words we say; only His Presence, which loves us and saves us, can interest it. Let apostolic fervor be renewed so that it might bear witness to Him who loved us first."

8

The *Villas Miserias* and "The Imperialism of Money"

The austerity of the new pope has become prover-bial in Buenos Aires. Alberto Barlocci reported in the magazine *Popoli* that on the occasion of an inter-religious meeting, when the participants arrived at the Archbishop's residence, they found Bergoglio himself waiting for them at the front entrance, with-out any assistant. And he, with that sense of humor of his combined with a grain of truth, said to them, "What else is a cardinal supposed to do if not open doors?"

Archbishop Bergoglio's closeness to his people, par-ticularly the less well-to-do, the weakest, the poor, and the sick, was a distinctive feature of his episcopate. "He celebrated countless Masses for us, among the *cartoneros* (those who collect cardboard cartons from the trash), in the *villas miserias* (shanty-towns), among the unemployed", comments Emilio Persico, a member of parliament who is strongly committed to social reform. "He always had something to say to us."

Bergoglio always proved to be close to the Church that stands "on the frontier" and sent priests into the *villas miserias*, arranging for their training, supporting them, and encouraging them. And especially visiting them. This closeness of his to the people and his words about poverty and social justice have often been interpreted, first by the government of Nestor Kirchner and then by that of his wife, the current president, Cristina, as a rebuke to the world of politics.

Annoyed because of his homilies for the *Te Deum* in May in the cathedral of Buenos Aires, commemorating the revolution for independence, the Kirchners preferred to be in other dioceses for that occasion. So as not to find Bergoglio.

The future pope used strong words to describe the situation of the Argentine capital: "In Buenos Aires, slavery has not been abolished. Here there are people who still work as the slaves used to work", he said in the presence of members of the nongovernmental organization La Alameda, a group of activists against the sexual exploitation of women and against slave labor in the many clandestine textile workshops or among the migrant workers who arrive from neighboring countries to harvest grapes or to pick fruit.

December 30, 2004, a scorching day at the close of the year in Buenos Aires, ended tragically with a fire in the Cromañon nightclub, where a rock concert was being held. The deadly conflagration, which started when someone lit a flare, spread with lightning speed: when it was over, around one hundred were dead and hundreds suffered from smoke inhalation. The city, once again, was struck severely by the lack of oversight, by corruption, and by irresponsibility: the managers of the club had been keeping the security exits chained shut. "Bergoglio", writes Alberto Barlocci in *Popoli*, "wanted the Church to show solidarity in this moment of sorrow. For many persons affected by the tragedy, this close presence was a consolation, and for some, it was nothing less than the rediscovery of a faith they seemed to have lost. For many, it was an encounter with a Church that is near, like a friend, a sister and mother."

"The same thing happened in February of the following year, when negligence, irresponsibility, and corruption caused the tragedy at the Once railroad station, right in the civic center: fifty-one dead and hundreds wounded. On that occasion, too, the Archbishop of Buenos Aires was able to place the Church at the service of the poor people compelled to travel on public transportation in very bad conditions."

At the beginning of the new millennium, Argentina experienced economic-financial collapse. In

December 2001, the country was wracked with serious social disorders: many families ended up on the streets. One day, from a window of the bishop's residence, Bergoglio, just created a cardinal, saw the police on the Plaza de Mayo beating a woman. The Archbishop picked up the telephone and called the Minister of the Interior. They did not put him through but had him speak to the Secretary of Security. Bergoglio asked whether he knew the difference between agitprop and people who were simply asking to get their own money, which was being held back by the banks.

The future pope spoke about that period in January 2002, in a long interview with Gianni Valente published in *30Giorni*. Describing the situation, Bergoglio recalled that the Argentine bishops had spoken to the people about many aspects of this

unprecedented crisis: the magical concept of the State, the squandering of the people's money, extreme liberalism through the tyranny of the market, fiscal irresponsibility, lack of respect for the law both in the observance and in the way in which it is framed and applied, the loss of the sense of work. In a word, general corruption that undermines the nation's cohesiveness and diminishes its prestige in the sight of the world. This is the diagnosis. And at bottom, the root of the Argentine crisis is one of morality.

There was in that time a real economic and financial terrorism. Which produced effects that can easily

125

be documented, such as an increase in the number of the rich, an increase in the number of the poor, and the drastic reduction of the middle class. And other less economic consequences, such as the disaster in the field of education. Right now, in the city and in the residential areas around Buenos Aires, there are two million young people who neither study nor work. Given the barbaric way in which economic globalism has been accomplished in Argentina, the Church of this country has always looked to the guidelines of the Magisterium. Our points of reference are, for example, the criteria clearly set forth in the Post-Synodal Apostolic Exhortation by John Paul II, *Ecclesia in America*.

More than eighty years ago, in the encyclical *Quadragesimo anno*, written shortly after the stock market crisis in 1929, Pope Pius XI had described as "the international imperialism of money" the speculative economic model that was capable of impoverishing millions of families in an instant. Bergoglio considered this

an expression that never loses its relevance and that has biblical roots. When Moses goes up the mountain to receive God's law, the people commit the sin of idolatry by fashioning a golden calf. The present-day imperialism of money, too, shows an unmistakably idolatrous face. It is odd how idolatry always travels together with gold. And wherever there is idolatry, God is written off, along with the dignity of man, made in the image of God.

126

Thus, the new imperialism of money gets rid of labor, of all things, which is the way in which man's dignity is expressed, his creativity, which is the image of God's creativity. A speculative economy no longer has need even of labor; it does not know what to do with labor. This leads to the idol of money that is produced by itself. And so there are no obstacles to transforming millions of workers into unemployed persons.

This judgment on reality was derived by the bishops from the social teaching of the Church and from the major documents of the Latin American episcopate.

Important in this connection are the Pueblo documents. The Conference of the Latin American Bishops in Pueblo marked a watershed. They succeeded in looking at Latin America through a dialogue with its own cultural tradition. And also with respect to the political and economic systems, the good that they had at heart was the whole wealth of religious and spiritual resources of our peoples, which are expressed, for example, in the popular devotions that Paul VI had already praised in his Apostolic Letter *Evangelii nuntiandi* in no. 48.

The Christian experience is not ideological; it is marked by a non-negotiable originality, which springs from amazement at the encounter with Jesus Christ, from marveling at the person of Jesus Christ. And our people preserve this, and they manifest it in popular piety. Both the leftist ideologies and this now triumphant economic imperialism of money write off the

Christian originality of the encounter with Jesus Christ, which so many of our people still live in the simplicity of their faith.

He had harsh words also about the role played by the international community and by central financial institutions: "It seems to me that they do not put man at the center of their reflections, notwithstanding the fine words. They always point out to the governments their strict guidelines, they always talk about ethics and transparency, but they appear to me like ethicists without goodness."

As a standard by which to address the crisis, the future pope declared:

> In becoming involved in this common attempt to overcome the crisis in Argentina, keep in mind what is taught by the tradition of the Church, which regards oppressing the poor and defrauding workers of their wages as two sins that cry out to God for vengeance. These two traditional expressions are utterly relevant in the magisterium of the Argentine episcopate. We are tired of systems that produce poor people so that then the Church can support them. The response of the bishops in this emergency has been to open in the parishes a network of food programs for children and for the ever-increasing numbers of people who live on the street. The Catholic hierarchy has also agreed to become involved at the table of reconciliation, while taking good care to assume the role of a moral entity.

"We have all sinned", the President of the Bishops' Conference, Estanislao Esteban Karlic, had said.

"We are part of our people," Bergoglio noted, "and we share with them in sin and in grace. We can proclaim the gratuitousness of God's gift only if we have experienced that gratuitousness in the forgiveness of our sins. In 2000 the Argentine Church is observing, publicly too, a time of penance and of asking society for forgiveness, also in reference to the years of the dictatorship. No sector of Argentine society has asked pardon in the same way."

The Church, the Cardinal concluded, has always invited people "to seek dialogue among the parties in society", has participated in the national dialogue, even though she was not the one to initiate it or to conduct it: "The Church offers the space for dialogue, like someone who offers his house so that two brothers can meet and be reconciled. But she is not one sector, a lobby, a party that participates in the dialogue side by side with other interest and pressure groups."

And at a moment when the leading class found itself totally discredited, the future pope explained: "We need to vindicate the importance of politics, even though politicians have discredited it, because, as Paul VI said, it can be one of the highest forms of charity. In our country, for example, the functionalist mentality connected with the prevailing

129

economic model has done its experiments on the two extremes of life, children and the elderly, the two phases of life most affected by crises, causing devastating effects in the fields of education, health care, and social welfare. And a people that does not care for its children and its elderly has no hope."

Bergoglio seemed to have clear ideas about how Argentina would overcome the crisis: "I believe in miracles. And Argentina has a great and beautiful people. These spiritual resources preserved by our people are already the beginning of a miracle. And I agree with Manzoni, who says, 'I have never found that the Lord started a miracle without finishing it well.' I expect that he will finish well."

"The story is told", we read in the book *El Jesuita*, "about one of his frequent visits to the *villas* of Buenos Aires. During a meeting with a group of men of the parish . . . a bricklayer stood up and told him with emotion: 'I am proud of him, because whenever I passed by here, with my co-workers, I always saw him sitting in one of the last rows, like anyone else.' "

The explosion of joy in the *villas miserias* over the election of Father Bergoglio was tremendous: "Now the lowly have a friend in Rome."

In order to understand Pope Francis, we need to start from these *villas*, from the garage covered with murals that houses the parish of Nuestra Señora de

Caacupé. This is the church of the Paraguayan immigrants dedicated to the Blessed Virgin, just as in Charrúa there is Our Lady of Copacabana venerated by the Bolivians or the Argentine Virgin of Luján. "The last time Bergoglio was here", Padre Toto reminisced to *La Stampa*, "was December 8 of last year. He never missed the feast of Our Lady. He was at home here: he used to celebrate Mass, administered the sacraments, even blessed photos, and then ate with us *el locro*", the thick soup made of meat and corn that is prepared in the open air on such occasions.

Jessica Araujo cannot keep back the tears when she remembers what happened last November 10: "First Communion of my son Maxi. You know how it is: I got pregnant at age fifteen. It changed my life and forced me to quit school. Then in comes this gentleman dressed in civilian clothes: he must have taken the bus, because I saw no cars outside. Then he vested as a priest, and now I recognized him: Padre Jorge, here to give First Communion."

There are dozens like her in the little office of the parish with the corrugated metal roof: one of these young ladies shows the photo of the then-cardinal with her husband at evening marriage instruction sessions, another, a picture of a young blind girl being confirmed. "One of us," insists Padre Toto, reminiscing about the new pope to the correspondent from *La Stampa*, Paolo Mastrolilli:

A religious man from the heart, with no tinsel. Imagine: yesterday he called the archbishop's chancery to wish an employee a happy birthday. The poor woman got upset and stammered, "Now I do not even know how to address you!" And he said: "Padre Jorge, right?" When I went into his office, I happened to see the packages of spaghetti near the desk, because in fact he used to eat there and often cooked for himself. The last time I looked for him, before the conclave, I needed his signature on an urgent document: "All right," he told me, "but you have ten minutes' time to explain it all to me, because I am leaving for Rome."

The face of the Church "of nearness", which becomes a neighbor to those who suffer, the face desired by Bergoglio, became a reality along these streets where the police are afraid to walk at night. "He was born in the popular district of Flores," a Franciscan friar named Carlos Trovarelli says, "and he never left off being a man of the people." "I saw with my own eyes", says Father Facundo Beretta Lauria, who is proudly "Calabrese", "how he reacted when the *narcos* (drug-dealers) threatened to kill my colleague Padre Pepe because he wanted to rid our streets of *el paco*, a cheap drug made with the residue of cocaine, which is given to small children. He spoke up and then told us: 'Call me any time, if there is anything that I can do for you, because I am going to follow this story personally.'"

Father Facundo, who wears sandals, jeans, and a clerical shirt with the collar unbuttoned, goes on to say: "Once there were misunderstandings: politics got mixed up with almost everything. Now, when we meet, Bergoglio always insists on the same thing: 'Never grow weary of being merciful.' And he is right, because when faith is joined to solidarity, then the festival begins even in the *villas miserias*."

However, when Jorge Mario Bergoglio became archbishop, in Buenos Aires there were, all told, only six *curas villeros*, that is, priests who go to live in the notorious districts and devote themselves to the people of the shanty-towns. "Now there are twenty-four of us," says Padre Facundo, "because he supports us personally and comes to work in the middle of the street with us. He celebrates Masses for the prostitutes in the Plaza Constitución, visits the AIDS patients, and also keeps in contact with the families of the *desaparecidos*, always hoping that at least the truth will set us free. As Pope Francis said, though, we are not a non-governmental organization, and all this is done in the name of the principles of the faith."

In 2009, when one of these priests, Padre Pepe, was threatened by the drug traffickers, Bergoglio defended him. In an interview published by *30Giorni*, he said concerning the *cura villeros*: "They work and pray. They are priests who pray. And they work in

133

catechesis, in social programs. . . . This is what pleases me. They say about that parish priest who was threatened, and it is true, that he has a special devotion to Don Bosco. It is precisely Don Bosco's style that moves me."

How much good these pioneering priests do, supported and loved as they are by their bishop who has become the pope, can be seen in the eyes of Miriam, a beautiful young woman who a few years ago used to sleep among the dumpsters. They had taken away her two babies, and she spent her time looking for money for *el paco*, drugs. She looked for it in every way possible. "I thought there was no more salvation for me. But in the streets I kept meeting the priest, who would tell me: 'God loves you.' Now I work as a catechism teacher and want to become a therapy aide for drug addicts who want to be cured."

During Holy Week in 2008, Cardinal Bergoglio decided to come celebrate the Mass of the Lord's Supper in the *villas miserias*, and he washed the feet of twelve youths from the Hogar de Cristo, the rehabilitation center for drug addicts where the priests of the *villas*, witnessing to the Gospel of Mercy, give hope back to the desperate.

9

Francis, the Reasons for a Name

On Thursday, March 14, on the morning of his first day as Bishop of Rome, Francis concelebrated Mass in the Sistine Chapel together with the cardinals who had elected him. He did not want to give the programmatic speech that the Secretariat of State, as is the tradition, had written ahead of time for the new pope. He set it aside. There will be time for programs. The 266th Bishop of Rome, elected after a lightning-fast conclave, spoke off the cuff, commenting on the Scripture readings. He decided to preach standing, at the ambo, without the miter on his head, as pastors do, instead of reading a homily while seated in the presider's chair. He leafed through the pages of the Gospel and with simplicity uttered profound, radical words, warning the Church about the danger of spiritual worldliness, which the new pope has always considered "the worst sin in the Church".

Francis' first papal Mass already signaled the change that is taking place. The new pope did not put on the precious and increasingly tall gold-embroidered miters that had reappeared in recent years among the papal vestments. He used a simple one made of cloth, the same one that appears in so many images of his Masses with the most abandoned people in the *villas miserias*, the shanty-towns of Buenos Aires. The people who have always seen in him the face of a Church "of closeness" that is capable of "transmitting and facilitating the faith", of giving hope. As of March 14, the papal masters of ceremonies, too, in the name of renewed Franciscan sobriety, which had already been foreshadowed the previous evening with the decision not to put on the red *mozzetta* lined with ermine, have put back in the drawer the vestments ornamented with lace.

A simple Mass, therefore. Celebrated *per Ecclesia*, for the Church. Beneath the dramatic spectacle of *The Last Judgment* by Michelangelo, the fresco that in the preceding hours the cardinal electors had had before their eyes while they slowly walked, in a line, each one holding his paper ballot in plain view in his hand, to cast their votes to elect the successor of Peter.

There was suspense about what the new pope would say. Traditionally the Secretariat of State prepares in advance a rough draft of a speech for this first papal homily, so as to present some programmatic

136

point, usually pertaining to the major themes in the life of the Church. The text is revised and completed by the newly elected pope and then declaimed in the Sistine Chapel several hours later. So it happened in 2005 with Benedict XVI, and so it had happened in 1978 with John Paul I and John Paul II. Pope Bergoglio chose to do it differently. He decided not even to take into consideration the prepared discourse, which according to tradition was in Latin. And he preached off the cuff. Another sign. Francis reflected on the three verbs "to journey", "to build", and "to profess", taking them from the respective readings of the Mass. He recalled the first instructions given by God to Abraham: "Walk in my presence and live blamelessly." He invited his listeners to walk "in the presence of the Lord, in the light of the Lord, seeking to live with the blamelessness that God asked of Abraham in his promise". Words addressed first of all to the cardinals, to the Roman Curia, to all the faithful.

Then he spoke about building the Church, about stones that "are solid", about "living stones, stones anointed by the Holy Spirit". He recalled that it is necessary "to build the Church, the Bride of Christ, on the cornerstone that is the Lord himself". Finally, profess the faith. "We can walk as much as we want, we can build many things, but if we do not profess Jesus Christ, things go wrong", Pope Bergoglio said.

"We might become a charitable NGO, but not the Church, the Bride of the Lord."

A reference to the risk run by the Church of transforming herself into a charitable organization was contained also in the homily in the Mass *pro eligendo Pontifice* presided over by the Cardinal Deacon Angelo Sodano in Saint Peter's two days earlier. The comparison is, in the first place, a reference to the Magisterium of Benedict XVI, the "Bishop Emeritus" of Rome (as the new pope rechristened him on the evening of his election), who had several times warned against restricting the term charity "to solidarity or simple humanitarian aid", whereas evangelization is the most important "work of charity".

If it is not built "on stone", the new pope continued, then we have "the same thing that happens to children on the beach when they build sandcastles: everything is swept away, there is no solidity." Francis then cited the words of [the late nineteenth-century French novelist] Léon Bloy: "Anyone who does not pray to the Lord, prays to the devil." He then commented: "When we do not profess Jesus Christ, we profess the worldliness of the devil, a demonic worldliness."

Journeying, building, professing. It is not always easy, the Pope acknowledged, "because in journeying, building, professing, there can sometimes be jolts, ... movements that pull us back." Even Peter, the same Peter "who professed Jesus as Christ", tells him: "I will follow you, but let us not speak of the Cross." And then Pope Francis uttered the most dramatic and radical words: "When we journey without the Cross, when we build without the Cross, when we profess Christ without the Cross, we are not disciples of the Lord, we are worldly: we may be bishops, priests, cardinals, popes, but not disciples of the Lord." He spoke then about the danger of a spiritual worldliness, about the danger of a Church that, if she does not witness to Christ and his Cross, can become an obstacle to evangelization.

"My wish is that all of us, after these days of grace," the new pope went on to say simply, "will have the courage, yes, the courage, to walk in the presence of the Lord, with the Lord's Cross; to build the Church on the Lord's blood which was poured out on the Cross; and to profess the one glory: Christ crucified. And in this way, the Church will go forward." A Church that, in order to resume her journey forcefully, cannot forget the Cross and must be ready to follow her Lord to the point of martyrdom.

On Friday, March 15, Francis received the cardinals in an audience in the Clementine Hall. And through them he addressed the whole Church, urging them: "Let us never yield to pessimism, to that bitterness that the devil offers us every day." It was a cordial, extended meeting, in which the cardinals over the age of eighty, who had been excluded from the conclave, also participated. The Pope arrived and sat on his throne. His unusual black shoes stood out against his white clothing. He listened to the greeting of the Dean, Angelo Sodano, and, when he stood up, impulsively, to go greet him, he overlooked the steps and nearly slipped. Then he spoke, reading a text to which he made several impromptu additions, citing from memory a Father of the Church in Latin and the German poet Hölderlin in the original language. He said that he had found his first encounter with the crowd after the election "deeply moving". He dedicated heart-felt words to Benedict XVI, emphasizing particularly "his humility and his meekness", two characteristics with which Francis appears to be completely attuned.

In speaking to the prelates, he always called them "brother Cardinals" and emphasized the beauty of the experience that they had had during the days of the conclave: "That community, that friendship, that closeness that will do us all good. And our acquaintance and mutual openness have helped us to be docile to the action of the Holy Spirit." Francis recalled that the Spirit himself "creates all the differences among the Churches, almost as if he were an Apostle of Babel. But on the other hand, it is he who creates unity from these differences, not in 'equality', but in harmony."

The Pope takes a positive view: "Let us never yield to pessimism, to that bitterness that the devil offers us every day. Let us not yield to pessimism or discouragement: let us be quite certain that the Holy Spirit bestows upon the Church, with his powerful breath, the courage to persevere and also to seek new methods of evangelization, so as to bring the Gospel to the uttermost ends of the earth." There was encouragement, too, for the "half of us" who "are advanced in age": "Let us pass on this wisdom to the young: like good wine that improves with age."

Cordial with them all, as he met the cardinals one by one, the Pope smiled, joked, and answered their questions, and to each one who kissed his hand, he responded by doing the same. Almost none of the prelates wore a pectoral cross of gold. The Franciscan style is evidently catching on. He spoke at length with Cardinal Marc Ouellet, but also with the President of the Governatorate Giuseppe Bertello and with the Honduran Óscar Rodríguez Maradiaga. Several African prelates asked him to bless rosaries and sacred objects, and Cardinal Fox Napier offered him a yellow plastic bracelet connected with a benefit project, which Francis immediately put on his wrist.

After lunch in the Casa Santa Marta, which he ate once again with the cardinals, changing his table each day, without a prearranged place for him, Francis decided to leave the Vatican to go visit his friend,

141

the ninety-year-old Argentine Cardinal Jorge Mejía, who had suffered a heart attack two days earlier. At the Pius XI Clinic on the via Aurelia he chatted with him for a half hour, then blessed the hands of the cardiologist and greeted the physicians and patients.

This visit recalled the one made by John Paul II on the day after his election, October 17, 1978, when he went to the Gemelli Clinic to visit his friend Bishop Andrzej Deskur.

The Vatican bureaucracy, while awaiting the reappointment of the heads of dicasteries and considering the change of its team of collaborators, lives from day to day. For the initial period, Pope Francis selected as his private secretary Alfred Xuereb from Malta, the former second secretary of Benedict XVI. Everyone from beyond the Tiber has to get used to the new style of a pope who prefers to ride the bus with the cardinals instead of using the official limousine. A Bishop of Rome who, despite having ascended to the throne, would like to change as little as possible of his way of living and witnessing to the Gospel. In a single stroke, some displays and rituals of the papal court seem to belong to a bygone era.

Confirmation of the new style, along with a note about the reasons for the choice of the name Francis, was provided on Saturday, March 16, at the audience in Paul VI Audience Hall for the more than six thousand journalists, cameramen, and technicians who had been accredited to cover the conclave. The pope once again abandoned the text of his prepared speech. And he spoke compelling words that are almost a program for his pontificate.

For the new pope, the occasion for expressing this desire is his explanation of his choice of name [see pp. 66 ff. above]. Pope Francis also asked the journalists who report on the life of the Church never to forget the dimension of faith. He invited them to try to "understand more fully the true nature of the Church ... and to know the spiritual concerns which guide her". And he told them to pay particular attention to what is true, good, and beautiful: "This is something which we have in common, since the Church exists to communicate precisely this: Truth, Goodness, and Beauty 'in person'."

Among the remarks added off the cuff, Francis recalled that "Christ remains the center, not the Successor of Peter.... Christ is the center.... Without him, Peter and the Church would not exist or have reason to exist." In short, the Pope is not the main actor. The meeting with the journalists concluded with an "I love all of you very much."

Another breath of fresh air then wafted through the two papal events scheduled one after the other on Sunday. In the morning at 10:00, Francis decided to celebrate Mass in the little Church of Saint Anna

143

located within the Vatican, although it is the parish for the Romans who live in Borgo Pio. The Pope gave an impromptu homily that can be described as his first great encyclical: "And Jesus has this message for us: mercy. I think—and I say it with humility—that this is the Lord's most powerful message: mercy."

We live in a society that makes us less and less accustomed to acknowledge our responsibilities and to take charge of them: indeed, it is always other people who are wrong. The others are always the immoral ones; it is always their fault, never ours. But we sometimes experience also a certain return of clericalism intent only on "regularizing" the lives of persons through the imposition of preliminary requirements and prohibitions that suffocate freedom and weigh down everyday life, which is already so wearisome. Quick to condemn rather than to welcome. Able to judge but not to bend down to the miseries of mankind. The message of mercy, the heart of this first unwritten encyclical of the new pope, demolishes both clichés at the same time.

Pope Francis commented on the Gospel passage about the adulterous woman whom the scribes and Pharisees intended to stone, as prescribed by the Mosaic law. Jesus saves her life, demanding that the one who was without sin should cast the first stone: they all went away. "Neither do I condemn you; go and sin no more."

The first and only step required to experience mercy, Francis explained, is to recognize the one who is in need of mercy. "[Jesus] comes for us, when we recognize that we are sinners", he said. It is enough not to imitate the Pharisee who stood before the altar, thanking God that he was "not like other men". If we are like that Pharisee, if we think that we are just, "then we do not know the Lord's heart, and we will never have the joy of experiencing this mercy!" Someone who is used to judging others, thinking that he is all right, considering himself just and good, does not notice his need to be embraced and pardoned. And, on the other hand, there are those who notice it but think that they cannot be redeemed because they have done too much evil.

In this connection, the Pope repeated a dialogue that took place in the confessional when a man, hearing this word about mercy addressed to him, had replied to Bergoglio: "Oh, Father, if you knew my life, you would not say that to me ... I am a great sinner!" And the Cardinal replied: "All the better! Go to Jesus: he likes you to tell him these things! He forgets. He has a very special capacity for forgetting. He forgets, he kisses you, he embraces you; and he simply says to you: 'Neither do I condemn you; go and sin no more.' That is the only advice he gives you. After a month, if we are in the same situation ... let us go back to the Lord. The Lord never tires of forgiving: never! It is we who tire of asking his forgiveness. Let us ask for the grace not to tire of asking forgiveness, because he never tires of forgiving."

God never tires of welcoming and forgiving, if only we acknowledge that we are in need of his forgiveness. These simple, profound words of Pope Francis are a breath of fresh air. For so many. Precisely because they present the face of a Church that does not rebuke people for their frailties and their wounds, but cares for them with the medicine of mercy.

At the end of the Mass, Pope Francis wished to have at his side Padre Gonzalo, and he introduced this young Uruguayan priest who works with drug addicts. "Pray for him", he said. Then, unexpectedly, Pope Francis left the church, stood outside in front of the main entrance, and, like a simple parish priest, greeted one by one all those who had participated in the liturgy. Another simple, direct gesture. That was not enough: twice the Pope passed through the door of Saint Anna's, thus entering into Italian territory, in order to greet the faithful crowded up against the barriers. Vatican security was anxious; obviously this pontiff has a style of his own and, above all, does not intend to let himself be put in a cage. Francis reluctantly left the people who kept shaking his hand. The Angelus, the first Angelus from the window of the office of the as yet unoccupied papal apartment, was waiting.

The Pope appeared on schedule. And the first thing that he said was: "Brothers and Sisters, good morning!" Saint Peter's Square was packed, as was also the via della Conciliazione and some of the side streets.

"After our first meeting last Wednesday, today I can once again address my greeting to you all! And I am glad to do so on a Sunday, on the Lord's Day! This is beautiful and important for us Christians: to meet on Sundays, to greet each other, to speak to each other as we are doing now, in the square. This square which, thanks to the media, has global dimensions."

The Pope commented on the Sunday Gospel: the story of the adulterous woman whom Jesus saves from a death sentence. "Jesus' attitude is striking: . . . we do not hear words of condemnation, but only words of love." It is so easy for us to become indignant over the sins of others, to ask for condemnation without making an examination of conscience. "God's face is the face of a merciful father who is always patient", Francis said. "He does not tire of forgiving us if we are able to return to him with a contrite heart", he added. It is a matter of acknowledging that we are in need of forgiveness and realizing that there are no sinless people.

And immediately it was obvious that the message of mercy would be central in his pontificate.

Pope Bergoglio said that he was struck, on this subject, by a book by Cardinal Kasper. Here, too, he interrupted his prepared speech and joked: "Do not think I am promoting my cardinals' books."

But the book, he added, "did me a lot of good. . . . Mercy . . . changes the world, . . . makes [it] less cold and more just." He cited the Prophet Isaiah: "Even if our sins were scarlet, God's love would make them white as snow." To a world that finds it so difficult to believe, the new pope wanted to shout the same proclamation as two thousand years ago, that this mercy is not a sentiment but a person. His very striking way of recalling the Incarnation—the Angelus actually commemorates the Incarnation—was a maternal gesture: he held his arms in front of him and moved them as though rocking a baby and said, "Our Lady . . . held in her arms the Mercy of God made man."

The Pope told about an old lady who had gone to confession when he was Bishop in Buenos Aires, during a Mass celebrated in the presence of the Pilgrim Virgin Statue of Our Lady of Fatima. " 'We all have sins . . . [but] the Lord forgives all things', she said to me with conviction. 'But how do you know, Madam?' 'If the Lord did not forgive everything, the world would not exist.' I felt an urge to ask her: 'Tell me, Madam, did you study at the Gregorian [Pontifical University]?' " Francis recalled that we too should "learn to be merciful to everyone", and twice, before his final greeting, he repeated: "Let us not forget this word: God never tires of forgiving, but at times we get tired of asking for forgiveness." A plea not to give in to desperation.

On Tuesday, March 19, under sunny skies, Pope Francis solemnly began his pontificate. The liturgy was simple, but all in Latin. For the first time, the Ecumenical Patriarch of Constantinople attended, Bartholomew I. In the front row there was also the Rabbi of Rome, Riccardo Di Segni. The Pope came out onto the square three-quarters of an hour beforehand to ride back and forth across it in a white jeep, so as to be able to greet everyone. He told it to stop when he noticed a seriously ill person in the crowd. He got down to console the man and gently caressed him. At the beginning of the ceremony, he received the papal pallium, the stole made of lamb's wool that symbolizes the sheep carried on Jesus' shoulders, and a new ring, made of gold-plated silver.

Anyone who was expecting the Mass at the beginning of his pontificate to include a major programmatic homily was surprised. Pope Francis spoke about the faith, strength, and tenderness of a saint to whom he is very devoted and whom the Church was celebrating on that very day: Saint Joseph. He is the model whom the new Bishop of Rome wants to take as his inspiration.

Let us never forget that authentic power is service, and that the Pope too, when exercising power, must

149

enter ever more fully into that service which has its radiant culmination on the Cross. He must be inspired by the lowly, concrete, and faithful service which marked Saint Joseph and, like him, he must open his arms to protect all of God's people and embrace with tender affection the whole of humanity, especially the poorest, the weakest, the least important.... Only those who serve with love are able to protect!

This is the program of his pontificate: "to serve" humbly, returning to the essentials, so as to communicate the message of the mercy of a God who sacrificed himself on the Cross. To serve concretely. And then "to protect", opening his arms, tenderly welcoming all of mankind, especially the poor, the lowly, the weak.

After turning his thoughts to his predecessor, Joseph Ratzinger, who was celebrating his name day, and after greeting the delegations present, mentioning explicitly the representatives of the Jewish community, the new pope in his homily dealt with the figure of Saint Joseph. Standing as he preached, without the miter on his head, he emphasized that the mission entrusted by God to the carpenter of Nazareth was the mission to be a "protector".

Joseph lived out his vocation as protector "by being constantly attentive to God, open to the signs of God's presence and receptive to God's plans, and not simply to his own." He allowed himself to be "guided

150

by [God's] will; and for this reason he is all the more sensitive to the persons entrusted to his safekeeping. He can look at things realistically, he is in touch with his surroundings, he can make truly wise decisions."

Christians, like Joseph, protect Christ in their lives "so that we can protect others, so that we can protect creation". But Pope Francis recalled that the "vocation of being a 'protector'" involves everyone, not just Christians. "It means protecting all creation, the beauty of the created world. . . . It means respecting each of God's creatures and respecting the environment in which we live. It means protecting people, showing loving concern for all, and for every person, especially children, the elderly, those in need, who are often the last we think about."

The Pope continued, "It means caring for one another in our families: husbands and wives first protect one another, and then, as parents, they care for their children, and children themselves, in time, protect their parents. It means building sincere friendships in which we protect one another in trust, respect, and goodness. In the end, everything has been entrusted to our protection, and all of us are responsible for it."

"Whenever men fail to live up to this responsibility, . . . the way is opened to destruction and our hearts are hardened." In every period of history, the Pope said, "there are 'Herods' who plot death, wreak havoc, and mar the countenance of men and women." There-fore, Francis asked "all those who have positions of responsibility in economic, political, and social life", and also all men and women, to be " 'protectors' of creation, protectors of God's plan inscribed in nature, protectors of one another and of the environment. Let us not allow omens of destruction and death to accompany our world's journey!"

But in order to be able to protect, Francis explained, it is necessary not to allow "hatred, envy, and pride" to defile our lives. The Pope mentioned the word tenderness six times. Protecting and caring "demands goodness; it calls for a certain tenderness." And ten-derness, he concluded, "is not the virtue of the weak but rather a sign of strength of spirit and a capacity for concern, for compassion, for genuine openness to others." Therefore "we must not be afraid of good-ness and of tenderness!"

"To protect creation, to protect every man and every woman, to look upon them with tenderness and love, is to open up a horizon of hope; it is to let a shaft of light break through the heavy clouds."

Many, many people throughout the world recog-nize this look of tenderness and mercy on the face of the new pope.

10

What the Pope Will Be

With his simplicity and his frugality, which are neither a studied pose nor the product of a media strategy, Pope Francis has already sent in the first days of his pontificate an important signal of change. His rejection of the "flagship" of the Vatican fleet of automobiles, his reduction of the security detail that had ended up confining the pope, his decision not to move into the "papal" suite of the *Domus Sanctae Martae*, remaining instead in room no. 207, which had been assigned to him during the lottery of the cardinals' quarters before the conclave, and his intention to remain close to the people are already definite indications of it. An example that could lead to a sort of self-reform. Cardinals and bishops could begin to follow it. The enthusiasm with which the people—even those who were away from the faith or had never experienced the life of faith—welcomed the new pope and his initial messages is surprising. Some have cautioned that we should be wary of the media effect and of the deadly embrace from some secular commentators.

Those who are preoccupied with such things seem displeased that for once the Church and her message are attracting so many people, arousing interest, human sympathy, and admiration. And something more as well. Many people who were away from the faith have returned to the Church since the election of Bergoglio, struck by his words about mercy. The first great change, therefore, does not depend on Francis' new governing "team", or on a change of structures.

Obviously, this does not do away with the fact that a reform of the Curia is imperative and in all probability will be carried out. There are two aspects, in particular, of the necessary curial reform. The first is structural, involving a reform to streamline the Curia itself, with the combination and simplification of competencies. Various "pontifical councils" can be merged together. This would facilitate coordination among the dicasteries. The Curia, moreover, must not govern the Church but, rather, provide a service to the pope. Important also is the rapport between the Curia itself and the bishops' conferences, between the center and the periphery. A second aspect concerns the morality of the Curia itself, which in the past few years sometimes seemed to be in a decline: just look at the recent scandals, a certain way of handling questions related to finances, the existence of factions and interest groups. No one is ruling out, either, the possibility of eliminating the automatic inclusion of the heads of curial dicasteries in the College of Cardinals as a way of preventing careerism. Ecclesiastics must come to the Curia to work and to serve the pope, not to pursue a career.

In this connection, one may note the gradual loss of the traditional style of the Curia, which was that of capable, competent officials, who always remained behind the scenes, not taking sides, but ready to prepare a document or a memorandum or to dissect a problem with skills that are now disappearing.

This idea of reform is subordinate to the profile desired for the Church: in the wake of the purification begun by Pope Ratzinger, in order to evangelize, it is necessary to be credible.

The perspective of evangelization, Gospel simplicity, becomes the source of a real change and begins with liberation from the ballast and the burdens of certain curial customs. It is not impossible that some steps could be taken toward divorced-and-remarried Catholics: above all to make them feel loved, as children of the Church who, while not able to receive sacramental Communion, should be welcomed and made part of the community.

There has been discussion, since the election of Francis, of what his positions might be concerning some ethical topics, for example, with regard to the recognition of homosexual couples. The message of mercy and acceptance, which seeks to convey the reality of a God who is ready to welcome and pardon all, could inspire a different approach on this issue, too, without involving changes from the doctrinal perspective. Indeed, Bergoglio's critiques of attempts to equate same-sex unions with marriage are well known. Critiques that are founded on morality and the natural law.

Francis gave another important signal about his pontificate starting with his first appearance at the central balcony of Saint Peter's, when he repeatedly described himself as "Bishop of Rome". It is not difficult to imagine that precisely this bond with his diocese, with the Roman parishes, will be central for Francis. This emphasis on the dimension of the pontificate connected with the service of the Bishop of Rome may have interesting implications, both in the area of collegiality within the Catholic Church and also in the field of ecumenical relations, particularly with the Orthodox world. The presence of the Ecumenical Patriarch of Constantinople, Bartholomew I, at the inaugural Mass of the pontificate and the long fraternal dialogue that

Francis and the Patriarch had on that occasion are a promising sign.

Another work in progress from the preceding pontificate is the one concerning the Society of Saint Pius X. Bergoglio had spoken clearly about the traditionalist groups, which have a seminary and several churches in Argentina. "Paradoxically," he declared in an interview with Stefania Falasca published in *30Giorni* in 2007, "precisely because one remains [in the Church], precisely if one is faithful, one changes. One does not remain faithful, like the traditionalists or the fundamentalists, to the letter. Fidelity is always a change, a blossoming, a growth. The Lord brings about a change in those who are faithful to Him." On other occasions, the future pope had said that this type of very rigid religiosity will masquerade behind doctrines that pretend to offer justification but in reality deprive people of liberty and do not let them grow. It should also be added, however, that the Cardinal of Buenos Aires always stayed in contact with the local authority of the Society of Saint Pius X, meeting and engaging in dialogue with him, in a frank, sincere relationship. And, aside from bitter preemptive criticisms of the new pope dashed off by those who are nostalgic for the ermine and the red shoes, there are traditionalists who appreciate the many aspects connected to tradition found in the homilies and speeches of Francis, who on that first evening, just elected, had the faithful gathered on Saint Peter's Square pray the Our Father, Hail Mary, and Glory be and who never fails to speak about Mary and does not hide his devotion to the saints. And he intended to keep, although with greater restraint and simplicity, the essential characteristics of the Ratzingerian papal liturgies.

Interesting also are the developments in relations with Judaism. Bergoglio has always had good relations with the Jewish community and in 2010 co-wrote a book with the Chief Rabbi of Buenos Aires, Abraham Skorka (*Sobre el cielo y la tierra*, published by Editorial Sudamericana); it is a dialogue on many topics: God, atheists, religions and their future, disciples, prayer, sin, death, women, abortion, education, politics, money, the Holocaust, interreligious dialogue.

In the book, the future pope declares, "My hope in God is in the journey and in the quest, in allowing myself to search." Bergoglio looks at the world in terms of this experience. About the dialogue with atheists, he says: "When I meet atheists, I share human questions but do not pose the problem of God to them at first, unless they themselves pose it to me. If necessary, I tell them why I believe. The human dimension is something so rich to share that we can peacefully pool our wealth. Since I am a believer, I know that these riches are a gift from God."

In another passage, Bergoglio says: "I believe that someone who adores God has, as a result of his experience, the task of bringing about justice with his brethren. This is a very creative justice, because one must be inventive: education, social assistance, commitment, care for others, etc. For precisely this reason, a religious man is called a just man. In this sense, justice creates culture. The culture of an idolater and the culture of a woman or a man who adores the living God are not the same. Today, for example, we have idolatrous cultures in our society: consumerism, relativism, and hedonism."

Noteworthy also is another passage dedicated to the authority of religious leaders: "The great leaders of the people of God were men who left room for doubt. Moses was the meekest, most humble man on earth. In the sight of God, nothing matters except humility, and this requires religious leaders to allow room for God, to be familiar with the interior experience of darkness, of not knowing what to do. One of the characteristics of a bad leader is to be excessively authoritarian because of the confidence he places in himself." A position that Rabbi Skorka shares: "The [Jewish] faith itself is manifested by means of a certain sense of doubt. I can have 99.99 percent certainty about God but not 100 percent, because life is a search."

We find again in this book the teaching that the Church cannot be reduced to an agency for relief services. Bergoglio explains: "I maintain that a religious congregation cannot be compared to a non-governmental organization (NGO). The difference is its holiness: in an NGO, the word holiness does not enter into the equation. There is a suitable social behavior, there is honesty, there are ideas about how to complete a task, there is a political logic. The thing functions in a secular way. But in religion, holiness is inescapable for its leaders."

Also interesting is the reference to the pastoral experience of the Cardinal of Buenos Aires, which, in connection with the formation of candidates for the priesthood, recalls the choices made in his diocese: "We accept into the seminary only about 40 percent of those who apply. There may be, for example, a psychological phenomenon: pathologies or neuroses of persons who are looking for external security. Some who fail to attain fulfillment in life seek organizations that can protect them. One of these organizations is the clergy. We therefore keep our eyes open, we seek to know well the persons who show interest in the priesthood. Then, for an entire year, living together every weekend allows us to distinguish between those who have a vocation and those who are simply seeking a refuge or are mistaken in their perception of God's call."

One of the most moving passages of the dialogue, biblical scholar Father Matteo Crimello notes, is when the Rabbi and the Bishop address the topic of prayer. "Prayer should serve to unify people: it is a moment when we all say exactly the same words", declares Rabbi Skorka. Bergoglio agrees with that: "Praying is an act of freedom." And he adds: "Prayer is speaking and listening. There are moments of profound silence, of adoration, waiting for the time to pass."

The dialogue with the Rabbi also confronts the topic of the major ideologies of the twentieth century: "Christianity condemns with the same vehemence both communism and unbridled capitalism. A clear example is what happens with money that is deposited abroad. Money has a homeland, and someone who takes the wealth that is produced in one country so as to bring it somewhere else commits a sin, inasmuch as he does not honor the country that produces that wealth and the people who work to generate it." And he adds, with regard to the money-laundering that results from drug trafficking: "Blood-stained money cannot be accepted."

Significant also is the passage concerning the wealth of the Church: "They always talk about the wealth of the Vatican. A religion requires money to continue its operations, and if that money passes through banking institutions, this is not illicit. The money that goes into the accounts of the Vatican should be spent on lepers, on schools, on the African, Asian, and [Latin] American communities." Then, however, recalling the martyrdom of Saint Lawrence and his defense of the poor of Rome, he says: "The poor are the treasure of the Church, and we must take care of them. If we do not have that vision, we will build a mediocre, tepid Church with no strength." We can be sure that the IOR, too, the Istituto per le Opere di Religion (Institute for Works of Religion), if it continues to exist, will do so by thoroughly honoring its name, so that it will no longer lay itself open to accusations such as those of the last few decades.

As for the forms in which Christianity is present, in his dialogue with the Rabbi, Bergoglio says: "If you look at history, the religious forms of Catholicism are remarkably varied. We are thinking, for example, of the Papal State, in which temporal power was joined with spiritual power. It was a deformation of Christianity and did not correspond with what Jesus intended. Therefore, if in history there was such a major development, we can suppose that in the future the Church will adapt to the culture of her time. The dialogue between religion and culture is one of the keys to the Second Vatican Council. Another principle of the Church is continual conversion—*Ecclesia semper reformanda*—and her transformation assumes different forms over time, without changing the dogma."

There is no lack of anecdotes and witty remarks in the volume. One of these concerns whether or not priests should wear a cassock. Bergoglio quotes on this topic a conversation he had with a young priest to whom he said: "The problem is not whether or not you put it on but whether you roll up the sleeves to work for others."

The new pope also knows well the reality of the Evangelical sects, which are spreading more and more in Latin America. Luis Palau, one of the world leaders of Evangelical Christians, has told stories of his friendship with Bergoglio. And the pastor of Buenos Aires, Juan Pablo Bongarrá, recalls: "He asked us, too, to pray for him."

"[When you are with Bergoglio] you have the impression that he knows God the Father personally", Palau declared in an interview. "The way he prays, the way he talks to the Lord, is that of a man who knows Jesus Christ and is very spiritually intimate with the Lord. It's not an effort [for him] to pray."

The most interesting part of the interview is the one where he speaks about what the relationship between Pope Bergoglio and the Evangelicals might be like. "I think we will witness a papacy that will alleviate tensions. That does not mean that we will be in agreement about everything—that must be said immediately. He is the Pope of the Church of Rome, and there are questions on which we must confront one another and pray about, look for answers in the Bible.... There are doctrinal differences, but when there is an attitude of mutual openness and of listening to the Word of God, if it is taken seriously, then light comes from the Lord."

"The largest number of Catholics live in Latin America", Pastor Palau continues in the interview with *Christianity Today*, reprinted by the website *Vatican Insider*. "Even though millions of Christians have turned to Jesus Christ in an evangelically Christian way, no less than 70 percent of Latin America still would profess that they are Roman Catholics. Not many decades ago, there was a confrontational attitude, and it was not pleasant. There are a very few places where there is physical risk to believers, but nothing like it was fifty years ago. Now the tensions are more theological."

Palau thinks that with Pope Francis there will be no conflict: "He has proved it over and over in his term as a cardinal in Argentina. There was more building bridges and showing respect, knowing the differences, but focusing on what we can agree on: on the divinity of Jesus, his virgin birth, his Resurrection, the second coming." But beyond the theological positions, we should speak about the personal relations. Luis Palau recalls a meeting in which Bergoglio told him that on the staff of the archbishop's chancery he had an Evangelical Christian accountant: "I can trust him", he explained, because "we spend hours [together] reading the Bible and praying and drinking *maté* [an Argentine green tea]."

In February 2012, Benedict XVI had held his next-to-last consistory for the creation of new cardinals. It had been a very Italian and very curial consistory. On that occasion, Pope Ratzinger had given a homily calling for humility and a sense of service. Cardinal Bergoglio had not come to Rome. I reached him by telephone to ask him whether he could grant me an interview based on the words of the Pope, but also dealing with the particular situation that the Roman Curia was going through at that moment, with the Vatileaks scandal. The confidential documents stolen from the Pope's writing desk had already begun to emerge a month earlier, but nothing was yet known about the responsibility of the majordomo of Benedict XVI. We spoke a little by telephone. This is the transcription of my questions and his answers. The interview was published on the website *Vatican Insider*. As he always does at the end of a conversation with journalists, Bergoglio said to me, too: "Do you think the things I said to you can be of any use?"

What do you make of the Pope's decision to call for a Year of Faith and his insistence on the new evangelization?

Benedict XVI has insisted on the renewal of faith being a priority and presents faith as a gift that must be passed on, a gift to be offered to others and to be shared as a gratuitous act. It is not a possession, but a mission. This priority indicated by the Pope has a commemorative purpose: through the Year of Faith, we remember the gift we have received. And there are three pillars to this: the memory of having been chosen, the memory of the promise that was made to us, and the alliance that God has forged with us. We are called to renew this alliance, our belonging to the community of God's faithful.

What does evangelization mean in a context such as that of Latin America?

"The context is that which emerged from the fifth conference of Latin American bishops, held in Aparecida in 2007. It called us to undertake a continental mission: the entire continent is in a missionary state. Plans were and continue to be made, but the paradigmatic aspect remains: all ordinary activities of the Church take place with a view to the mission. This involves very strong tensions between center and periphery, between parish and district. We need to come out of ourselves and head for the periphery. We need to avoid the spiritual sickness of a Church that is wrapped up in her own world: when a Church becomes like this, she grows sick. It is true that going out onto the street implies the risk of accidents happening, as they would to any ordinary man or woman. But if the Church stays wrapped up in herself, she ages. And if I had to choose between an injured Church that goes out into the streets and a sick, self-enclosed Church, I would definitely choose the former."

What is your experience of this in Argentina and, in particular, in Buenos Aires?

We seek to make contact with families that are not involved in the parish. Instead of just being a Church that welcomes and receives, we try to be a Church that comes out of herself and goes to the men and women who do not participate in parish life, do not know much about it, and are indifferent toward it. We organize missions in public squares where many people usually gather: we pray, we celebrate Mass, we offer baptism, which we administer after a brief preparation. This is the style of the parishes and of the diocese itself. Other than this, we also try to reach out to people who are far away, via digital means, the Internet and text messaging.

In his speech during the Consistory and in his homily on Sunday, February 19, 2012, the Pope stressed the fact that the cardinalate is a service and that the Church does not make herself. What are your thoughts on these words of Benedict XVI?

I was struck by the image evoked by the Pope, who talked about James and John and the tensions between

the first followers of Jesus over who should be first.
This shows us that certain attitudes and arguments
have existed in the Church since the beginning. And
this should not shock us. The cardinalate is a service; it is not an award to be bragged about. Vanity,
boasting about oneself, is an attitude of spiritual
worldliness, which is the worst sin that can be committed in the Church. This statement is found in
the final pages of the book entitled *The Splendor of
the Church*, by Henri de Lubac. Spiritual worldliness
is a form of religious anthropocentrism that has
Gnostic elements. Careerism and the search for
advancement certainly come under the category of
spiritual worldliness. An example I often use, to illus-
trate the reality of vanity, is this: look at the pea-
cock; it's beautiful if you look at it from the front.
But if you look at it from behind, you discover the
truth. . . . Whoever gives in to such self-absorbed vanity is hiding an enormous poverty inside.

What, then, does the genuine service of a cardinal involve?

Cardinals are not NGO representatives, but servants
of the Lord, inspired by the Holy Spirit, who is the
One that makes the true differences among charisms
and, at the same time, brings them to unity in the
Church. A cardinal must be able to enter into the
dynamic of the different charisms and at the same

time look toward unity. Aware that the creator of both difference and unity is the Holy Spirit himself. A cardinal who does not enter this dynamic, in my view, is not the sort of cardinal that Benedict XVI is calling for.

11

A Life "Transfixed" by God's Look of Love

In the archbishop's chancery in Buenos Aires, the office of Cardinal Bergoglio, today Pope Francis, was almost smaller than the one of his secretary. He never wanted the archbishop's office, on the top floor: it might give a sense of power and superiority. In the palace, he occupied the same room he had when he was Vicar General of his predecessor, Cardinal Quarracino. "It is an extremely austere room", Sergio Rubin and Francesca Ambrogetti write in the book *El Jesuita*. There was a simple wooden bed and a crucifix that used to belong to his grandparents, Rosa and Giovanni. There was also an electric heater, because, although the building had central heating, Bergoglio did not allow it to function unless all the personnel who worked in the archbishop's chancery were present. A lady used to come every Tuesday to clean, but the Cardinal made his own bed every morning.

Across from the room was his personal chapel. And in an adjoining room was contained his library, full of books and documents. Among them there was a now discolored one that contains his profession of faith, written "in a moment of great spiritual intensity" shortly before he was ordained a priest.

I want to believe in God the Father, who loves me as a son, and in Jesus, our Lord, who has poured his Spirit into my life so as to make me smile and thus to bring me to the eternal kingdom of life.

I believe in my past, which was transfixed by God's look of love, and on the first day of spring, September 21, he led me to an encounter so as to invite me to follow him.

I believe in my suffering, sterile because of the egotism in which I take refuge.

I believe in the misery of my soul, which seeks to gorge itself without giving . . . without giving.

I believe that others are good and that I must love them fearlessly and without ever betraying them so as to seek any security of my own.

I believe in religious life.

I believe in wanting to love much.

I believe in dying daily, being consumed, which I flee, but which smiles, inviting me to accept it.

171

I believe in God's patience, which is welcoming and good like a summer night.

I believe that Papa [i.e., Mario Bergoglio] is in heaven together with the Lord.

I believe that Padre Duarte is there, too, interceding for my priesthood.

I believe in Mary, my mother, who loves me and will never abandon me. And I look forward to the surprise of every day, in which love, strength, betrayal, and fear will appear, which will accompany me until the definitive encounter with that marvelous face that I continually flee, although I do not know what it is like, but that I want to know and love. Amen.

The Padre Duarte mentioned in this profession of faith is none other than the priest who on that first day of spring heard the confession of the seventeen-year-old Jorge Mario in the parish church. An encounter that was decisive for his discovery of God's call.

The new pope is very devoted to Saint Thérèse of Lisieux. When he came to Rome as a cardinal for the duties associated with the congregations on which he served, he used to stop at the little church of Santa Maria Annunziata in Borgo—popularly called the "Annunziatina"—an oratory in Rome located on the Tiber as it flows by the Vatican, a few steps from Saint Peter's Basilica. Padre Bergoglio rediscovered it on the way, which he usually traveled on foot, from the clergy house on the via della Scrofa to the Vatican. There he would stop and pray.

In October 2002, the Franciscan Friars of the Immaculate, who have taken care of the church since 1998, had begun to notice the presence of a priest who, punctually at nine in the morning, stopped to pray with great recollection and devotion before the statue of Saint Thérèse of the Child Jesus and then went away. "He was not that young a priest," Father Rosario M. Sammarco relates on the Facebook page of the Franciscan Friars of the Immaculate, "but tall in stature and vigorous. He made you curious, both by the punctuality with which he arrived and also by his very devout and simple demeanor. To give you some idea of it, at the end his prayer, he used to do as many despised old ladies of our countries do: he touched the statue and kissed it. Our curiosity increased when the friars noticed once that the priest had a cassock with red buttons. A cardinal, then? But who could he be?"

One of the friars, Brother Anselmo M. Marcos, assigned to the sacristy, being curious, decided one day to go up to him to ask the devout pilgrim who he was. Padre Bergoglio introduced himself and said that he was the Cardinal of Buenos Aires.

The new pope, hosting a lunch for the President of Argentina on the eve of the inaugural Mass of his pontificate, gave her a white rose, symbol of his devotion to Saint Thérèse.

From the very first hours after his election, Francis personally telephoned his friends in Rome and in Buenos Aires. He invited some of the to the Mass at the parish of Saint Anna on Sunday, March 17. Among the telephone calls he made was one to Daniel, who runs the newsstand on the calle Bolivar, near the Plaza de Mayo, a few steps from the Cathedral in Buenos Aires. The Pope called him to thank him and to discontinue his subscription to the daily *La Nación*, which, together with the *Clarín*, is among the most widely read newspapers in Argentina. The man could not believe his ears and thought that it was a joke. "*Hola*, Daniel, Padre Jorge speaking," the Pope told him over the telephone on Monday, March 18. "Come on, Mariano, don't be an idiot, cut it out!" the news vendor replied, thinking it was a friend who was playing a joke. "Seriously, I am Jorge Bergoglio, and I am calling you from Rome. Thank you for your service over all these years, but now please stop delivering the newspaper to me", the Pope said. "It was a shock, I started to cry, I did not know what to say...", Daniel admitted. "I told him that I would miss him and asked him whether we would see him soon on this side [of the Atlantic].

He answered that for at least a short time it would be complicated, but he added that he would always be present", the news vendor concluded his story.

A pope who the day after his election goes to pick up his suitcase and pay the bill at the clergy guesthouse, who telephones friends, who continues to be himself in every way and for every occasion. To Sergio Rubin and Francesca Ambrogetti, the authors of the book-length interview *El Jesuita*, the future pope had said: "The truth is that I am a sinner whom the mercy of God has loved in a special way." And to the question of how he would describe himself, he had responded: "Jorge Bergoglio, priest."